SPLITTING
UP

SPLITTING UP

UP

A LEGAL AND FINANCIAL GUIDE TO SEPARATION AND DIVORCE

THIRD EDITION

DAVID GREEN

KOGAN
PAGE

First published in 1988
Second edition 1992
Third edition 1995

Kogan Page Limited
120 Pentonville Road
London N1 9JN

British Library Cataloguing in Publication Data

A CIP record for this book is available from the British Library.

ISBN 0-7494-1517 7

Typeset by JS Typesetting, Wellingborough, Northants.

Printed and bound in Great Britain by Clays Ltd, St Ives plc.

Contents

Preface

This new edition of *Splitting Up* – like previous editions – is designed to save you and your partner cost and anguish if your relationship founders. Living together relationships are covered as well as married relationships.

If you are married you will see how you can deal with a reasonably straightforward divorce yourselves.

Married or not you will find suggestions which may help you to decide what income and property you, your partner and your children should end up with, and whittle down the cost of deciding it. Along the way you will see how, left to its own devices, the gulf between the law and the way it is put into practice may aggravate that cost.

In family law, as in all law, cost thrives on delay and dispute. But our existing family law nourishes that cost systematically by offering no more than imprecise words about your children, your money, your property and your marriage, and by producing results which often seem to come out of a different book altogether.

You have enough disputes already, and can certainly do without the cost of more. So offering specific guidelines on practical problems is central to the purpose of this book. But it looks also to the environment in which your decisions will have to be made – to wills, inheritance, solicitors and their costs (with or without legal aid), and the courts themselves. It explains how you can make a will yourself and considers some special problems – how do new partners and children come into the picture and what happens to granny in her flat?

This is a book about law, not a law book. It does not require you to refer to anything else. But fundamental sections of Acts of Parliament, although summarised in the text, appear in full in the Appendices in case you wish to study the precise wording; and when the facts of cases are discussed, references are given to them, and to many others that illustrate specific points, in the notes at the end of each chapter. To help you in case you wish to read a full report, the law reports of *The Times* newspaper have been used where possible. Back numbers of *The Times* are more likely to be found in reference libraries than the various bound editions of the law reports.

This edition includes a new chapter wholly devoted to the Child

Support Agency. Chapter 3 covers rule changes already introduced as well as the proposals in the White Paper 'Improving Child Support' published 23 January 1995. Experience suggests that those proposals will be given legal effect. But at the time of writing implementation still lay in the future, and this edition would be too long delayed if held back until it was accomplished. Some changes are planned from April 1995, others not until after 1996/97. So remember that where Chapter 3 says 'from April 1995' or 'from 1996/97' it refers to *proposals*, and that those elements will only have legal effect if and when legislation brings them into force.

Unfortunately, even if fully implemented the White Paper is unlikely to end the chaos which hallmarked the Agency's first years. What the law needed was for the courts to continue to calculate maintenance (but with the principles which they have anciently evolved fleshed out – Chapter 6 shows how that might be done – so that everyone applied the same starting rules, even if exceptional cases then required discretionary fine tuning); and a new agency to enforce *payment* in the minority of cases where there was default.

What it has ended up with is an entirely new set of formulae which only cover part of the maintenance picture and are infernally complex (they combine all the finical detail of DSS means-tested, subsistence-level benefit techniques with quite arbitrary percentage top-ups for the better off); and a new agency which is unable even to enforce payment effectively because it is swamped by having to take on every family with children; and because its formulae produce such bizarre results there are vastly more defaulters. Giving the Agency's officials and the Child Support Appeal Tribunal (CSAT) limited discretion to depart from formula calculations in exceptional cases (proposed after 1996/97) is unlikely to cure such basic structural problems. The courts have training, experience and precedent as guides to the exercise of discretion. The Agency's officials do not. The CSAT may be adequately equipped, but it is soon likely to be overwhelmed by appeals.

Child Support is therefore likely to attract continued controversy. Meantime, much else in family law is also volatile. Law Commission proposals to change the grounds for divorce (noted in Appendix 4) still hang fire. And decided cases (accommodated in the main text) continue to change the emphasis, and sometimes the substance, of law and practice.

That said, the basic objective of this book is still to help you, not to inform lawyers. But since a bird's eye view of a field whose characteristics and dynamics can barely be imagined merely by studying the law is necessary to that objective, anyone interested in family law (lawyers included) is likely to find it useful – as they have previous editions.

David Green
Castle Morris
Haverfordwest
SA62 5EJ

January 1995

Stop press – March 1995

(1) Grounds for Divorce – see page 26 and Appendix 4, pages 195–6

Moves to change the grounds for divorce are slowly accelerating, and the Lord Chancellor intends to introduce a White Paper in May 1995. This is expected to mirror the Law Commission and Green Paper proposals summarised in Appendix 4 (pages 195–6) but not to result in changes to the law until 1997 at the earliest. If implemented, the proposals will change procedure (as outlined in Appendix 4) but are unlikely to affect the bases of decisions involving children, maintenance and property with which much of this book is concerned.

(2) Child Support – see above and page 39

The Government has introduced a Bill to implement the White Paper 'Improving Child Support', whose proposals are already covered in this book. The Bill follows the White Paper precisely.

(3) Pension Rights – see pages 71, 78, and 116–17

A House of Lords bill may change the emphasis on pension rights. The courts will have to take them into account and not just have regard to them as before. Under an amendment pension funds may also have to pay part of a pension direct to a divorced spouse, who will then benefit directly and not only if their former partner is still liable to pay maintenance. If that happens property transfer and clean break settlements will no longer need to allow for pensions (pages 71 and 78). But the amendment may not survive. It raises a host of practical problems which can only be solved if the courts are given power to split pensions between spouses. So far there is no sign of that power being granted.

Chapter 1

Introduction, General Warnings and Guidelines

Introduction

Sooner or later most of us marry. We set out with high hopes. We accumulate possessions. We have children. But many relationships then fail. One hundred and eighty thousand wives or husbands, with 160,000 children under 16 between them, petition for divorce every year. A third of all marriages end in divorce.

If a third of all cars of a particular type wrecked themselves, we would regard it as conclusive evidence that they contained some fundamental flaw. So it is hardly surprising that many couples have come to the same conclusion about marriage, dispense with it altogether, and just live together. But that does not guarantee success. There are no statistics for unmarried relationships but they also fail.

The law does not intrude as powerfully in the affairs of cohabitees as it does in those of married people. The courts can unscramble marriage settlements. But if unmarried people reach detailed agreements about the ownership of their property, the courts will enforce them. On the other hand, the law and the courts now deal with children in precisely the same way whether their parents were married or not. Cohabitation is not a relationship free of legal consequences.

Very few adults and even fewer children emerge unhurt from collapsed relationships. But the hurt which anyway accompanies the severing of accustomed ties is made worse when people find themselves adrift on a legal ocean of which they may have no knowledge, and on which many unsuspected storms lie in wait. Neither those who sever ties, nor those who have them severed, are likely to be immune.

If you have children, your problems start with them. They will usually hope, often desperately, that the clock can be put back so that they can have both parents living with them again. But if the clock is irreversible, they will have to live with one of you only: and both you and your former partner will have to wrestle with their disappointed hopes, apart from the severely practical problems of who is to have their day-to-day care, and who is to provide for them. Everyone's misery will be less if you can agree the practical problems. But, agreed or not, your family will still find itself in a new world of legal terms – parental responsibility, residence, contact, maintenance and maybe specific issues and prohibited steps orders.

Financial problems follow swiftly. What is to happen to the house which was your home? Who is to have the other possessions which you and your partner have acquired and which you both previously used without thought as to whose they were.

If you have children the Child Support Agency will calculate and enforce payment of their basic maintenance (Child Support) – see further Chapter 3. Under existing rules laid down by Parliament around half that maintenance is designed to support the parent with whom the children live. So, along with the children, that parent will also be supported (to the extent that Child Support requires) until all the children become independent. The fact that you reached a clean break settlement in the courts, or that the parent with whom the children live has remarried – or that you never married – makes no difference.

In many families Child Support mops up everything which can reasonably be paid for the maintenance both of children and the parent they live with. But in no family with children can any parent look sensibly at the rest of his or her position until it is known what Child Support will be payable. So an application to the Child Support Agency has to be the first financial move for parents.

But Child Support is not the end of the financial story. Child Support takes the first bite out of available maintenance. And the courts must take any Child Support payable into account in considering any additional orders. But subject to that the courts retain all their previous powers. So:

1. If you were married but have no children the courts may order one of you to maintain the other (see further Chapter 6).
2. If your means are such that you can afford more than Child Support allows, the courts may order additional maintenance for children, *and* for the parent with whom they live if you were married (see further Chapter 6).
3. Only the courts can make 'property sharing' orders – lump sum payments, transfers or settlements; and adults only qualify for such orders if they were married. But children may qualify whether or not their parents were married. And property sharing orders in

favour of children are increasingly being used to protect their interests because their unmarried parents do not qualify (see further Chapter 7).

4. Even if you were not married you may have made a financial contribution to property which you and your partner accumulated. If so, you may have claims on that property. Again only the courts can deal with that (see Chapter 7).

Mortgages and debts further complicate the position. Who is to pay them and to go on paying them? The Inland Revenue also throws in its two-pennyworth. What happens to your respective liabilities for income tax? What personal allowances and what allowances against mortgage interest may you now claim?

The Department of Social Security (DSS) also contributes. Who pays what National Insurance contributions? What happens to the child family allowance? What happens to pension rights? If incomes are drastically reduced, what additional support is available?

Last but certainly not least in the financial stakes, what is it all going to cost and who is going to pay it? What about legal aid?

Then there are the legal procedures. Do you attempt to deal with your problems with negotiated documents outside the courts or do you go to court? If you go to court, do you go on the basis of previously negotiated terms, with applications for agreed court orders, or do you go with swords drawn to fight it out in the hope that the best man or woman will win? Afterwards you may be concerned with applications for adoption, for permission to take a child out of the country, even for permission to change its name. How are these approached?

The chapters which follow aim to provide some of the answers to these questions.

But there are some things which no book can do. No book can say much which will be useful to you in coping with the emotional consequences of a failed relationship. Advice, however worthy, rarely penetrates the way people feel.

So if you come across passages in this book which suggest that you and your partner should calmly and rationally set about the task of agreeing the destiny of your children, incomes and property, do not imagine that this advice is offered simply because your future lives are likely to be happier if you do so. If you can agree the fundamentals, they will be. Any such agreement necessarily implies a mutual recognition that the relationship which brought you together has ended. And that is your only safe starting point for the rest of your life.

But the reason for advocating harmony in the liquidation of your relationship is far more mundane than that. The cost of fighting can absorb a staggering proportion of the resources which you both have and on which you, your partner and your children will have to depend in the future. The final cost cannot be known until it is all over. And who has to pay it is a lottery. But most probably both of you will end up paying, and in many cases the burden will fall on you equally.

So, while this book does not offer miracle cures for misery, it does focus sharply on those areas which make the misery worse – the mysteries which surround the financial, legal and procedural rules which come into play when relationships break down, and the costs which you will face if you choose to fight it out. The information given and the suggestions made should help you and your former partner towards an agreement. The words will not make you happy if you are *un*happy, but the practical advice may save you even greater hardship.

General warnings

Two questions crop up more often than any other when people seek advice about a crumbling relationship: 'What are my rights?' and 'What are my liabilities?' They reveal a touching and quite unjustified belief that English law contains precise answers to the practical problems which people face when their relationships fail, and that it can offer them some small island of certainty when everything else is in chaos.

Well, it does not, even where you might expect it to. In addition, there are problems which may not be immediately obvious to you in controlling the work which has to be done if you employ a solicitor. So let us look at some basic cautions.

Children

On questions of parental responsibility, residence, contact and maintenance of children the law requires the courts to treat the welfare of the children as the first and paramount consideration.[1] In practice, that is usually interpreted as meaning that if the mother of the children wants the general care and control of them, it is in their interest that they should reside with her. If that is the decision, parental responsibility and contact will be the normal lot of their father, whether or not the parents were married. But if the parents were not married a father may be less likely to obtain a contact order if the father's parent–child relationship was so tenuous that no significant relationship ever existed.

Money, property and costs

The married

When it comes to the money and property of married people – and apart from the Child Support Agency – English law lays down no more than a series of very general principles to which the courts must 'have regard' in making decisions.[2] There are no rules to define what percentage each partner should have or, short of death or remarriage, how long maintenance should be payable or what proportion, if any, should be allocated to children. There are certainly principles and percentages which individual lawyers use in advising on these problems and in making decisions in court, and these are discussed more fully in the chapters which follow. But virtually every lawyer has his own favoured yardsticks and these differ, sometimes substantially. So if a husband and wife each consult their own solicitor and each supply him with identical factual information, the difference in approach alone may result in entirely different answers to the questions, 'What are my rights?' or 'What are my liabilities?'

What then?

Conventionally, armed with their different answers, negotiations to close the gaps then ensue. If it proves impossible to reach an agreed conclusion, the problem then goes to court where another view often emerges. And if that view is taken to appeal, still more may follow.

While all this is happening, time is passing and costs are rising. An ever-increasing slice of the family's assets and income becomes committed to the cost of resolving in what proportion it shall share what is left. In extreme cases there may be nothing left at all.

Even judges bewail such consequences. One remarked, 'Care should be taken by counsel and solicitors in family proceedings not to dissipate assets available to the parties by the costs of the legal actions pursued.'[3] But the danger lies in the system itself and in the fact that once people are on the roller-coaster of legal proceedings it is extremely difficult to get off again before it finally grinds to a halt. You save cost if you and your partner can agree.

The unmarried

Costs and the desirability of agreement are as significant for unmarried couples who have lived together – cohabitees – as they are for the married. But the law gives them less to argue about. For example, when cohabitees separate neither has any right to claim maintenance against the other for themselves. Paradoxically, however, if one dies while they are still living together without making reasonable provision for the maintenance of the other, the survivor may be able to claim such provision from the deceased's estate.[4]

A cohabitee also has no general right to claim any fair or reasonable carve-up of the property which the parties have.[5] But if they bought a house or other property in joint names, they will be entitled to share the value of that property in any proportion specifically defined by the deeds under which it was bought; or maybe in the proportions in which they contributed to the cost if they bought merely as 'tenants in common'; or equally (so long as both survive) if they bought as 'joint tenants'.[6] These arcane phrases and their effect are explained on page 123.

If contributions of unmarried people to the cost of property come into the picture (they may with any contributor, for the rules do not apply only to those living together in heterosexual or other relationships) the contribution has to have a cash value. If it does not, cohabitees' and contributors' rights are no greater than those of married women before 1970. As to those the House of Lords ruled in 1968:

> 'The wife does not get a share in the house simply because she cleans the walls or works in the garden or helps her husband with the painting and decorating. Those are the sort of things which a wife does for the benefit of the family without altering the title to or the interests in property.'[7]

So, for the unmarried, caution at the start of any relationship may save much heartache later. If you are going to live with someone, remember the long-term significance of putting property in joint names, and of defining who has what share at the outset. Remember also the probable consequences of financial contributions and the fact that keeping precise and accurate records to evidence what has gone on may be an essential part of your security.

Legal aid

Legal aid is not free unless you end up with nothing. If you are granted legal aid, the Legal Aid Fund will pay your lawyer's costs up to the conclusion of the legally aided proceedings. These will not be known until everything is complete. When it is, however, then, under the rules laid down by Parliament, the Legal Aid Fund has first claim on anything of value which you have recovered or preserved as a result of the proceedings. So any costs which you do not recover – and that includes costs which are ordered against, but cannot be recovered from, your 'opponent' – come out of what you have achieved. You will rarely recover all your costs. In matrimonial cases you may not recover any costs at all. Legal aid does not allow you to forget costs (see Chapter 11).

Your solicitor

By law a solicitor is expected to exercise all the care of someone trained in his profession. If he does not and you suffer loss, he knows (even if you do not) that afterwards you may sue him for damages. So if you ask a solicitor to act for you, he is obliged to check and double-check everything. Even if you and your partner are quite satisfied that you each know everything about each other's financial position, your solicitors may still have to go through all the procedures which they would follow if you were both concealing information – at your cost, of course – before *they* can be sure.

So if, in the hope of controlling costs, you reach agreement, it is not enough merely to give your solicitor all the information. Suppose, for example, you have agreed all the details of income and property with your former partner, and each of you has given your solicitor a full and complete breakdown. Without more, the solicitors may still have to involve themselves in a stream of mutual enquiries to make sure that everything is covered and, where relevant, backed up by documents and valuations. Equally, you and your former partner, mindful of costs, may have agreed exactly how you want income and property to be carved up between you and may tell your solicitors how it is to be. But your solicitors have a duty to advise you, and unless you insist that they merely implement what you have agreed, they will be obliged to attempt to help you on your way to what *they* think it should be. The steps which solicitors must take to establish who has what, and who shall have what, are far and away the most costly part of the break-up for anyone who owns anything at all. You and your former partner can save yourselves that cost if you instruct your solicitors specifically to accept what you say and not to do any more than implement it. And for safety's sake, say this in writing if you are going to say it at all.

There are then two basic pieces of advice:

1. If, despite other disagreements, it is humanly possible for you to agree arrangements about your property and your income which make mutual sense for you and your children, all of you will be a great deal better off.
2. If you still need lawyers to deal with the mechanics of court proceedings – and that may be wise for reasons we shall come to when dealing with financial orders – make sure that both of you instruct your lawyers to implement what you have agreed and no more. Even the best of agreements will rapidly crumble if either party succumbs to a siren voice saying, 'Oh, I think I could get you more' or 'I think I could get you off with less.' If either bends to that approach, you are both straight back on the costs roller-coaster.

Guidelines

If you are to sort out the details yourselves, you still need some indication of where you should start – what your basic rights and liabilities might be. Finding this out is difficult when the law does not contain any guidelines and when judges, when they mention anything specific, almost as often qualify it by saying that there are no general rules and each case must be taken on its own.

For all that, however, specifics *are* used, and much of the material in this book devoted to maintenance, houses, and other financial and property matters is concerned with what generally may be expected to happen, and what the courts have said by way of general principle (while always denying that there are any general principles) in decided cases.

In addition, Scottish law has been braver than English. The Family Law (Scotland) Act 1985 has actually defined – for Scotland – what property should and should not be shared. It has also identified specific principles for dividing the proportion to be shared, and it has come to grips in specific terms with the question of how long maintenance should continue, even though it has not abandoned general principles as a guide to its calculation. Much of what is now specific in Scottish law finds support in English cases, even if there are also others which say something different, and many which say that they do not imply any general precedent. The position in Scotland is therefore also summarised.

Finally, of course, you and your partner can go to your own

solicitors, ask them for advice as to your rights and liabilities, compare that advice, and still save yourselves a great deal of cost by discussing how to close any gaps which separate that advice yourselves.

Because of the state of English family law it is impossible to guarantee that, if you follow the principles of English practice or Scottish law discussed in this book, you might not obtain more, or have to pay less, than if you took your case along the conventional route through solicitors' negotiations and court proceedings. But it is possible to say that, in the majority of cases, the cost of fighting about the differences will probably more than wipe them out.

A specific case by way of final cautionary example: in 1983, after a Court Registrar had decided that the respective shares of wife and husband in their home were £24,000 and £8,000 (75:25 per cent) the husband appealed. The Court of Appeal reduced the wife's share to £20,000 and increased the husband's to £12,000 (62.5:37.5 per cent).[8] The wife obviously lost out. But the chances are that additional costs wiped out all the husband thought he had gained as well.

Notes

1. Section 1 Children Act 1989; see also in Re *H* (a minor) (1990) *The Times* 20 June
2. Appendix 1: Section 25 Matrimonial Causes Act 1973
3. *Clark* v *Clark* (1988) *The Times* 31 March; and see *Evans* v *Evans* (1990) *The Times* 3 February
4. Inheritance (Provision for Family & Dependants) Act 1975; see Chapter 8
5. *Mossop* v *Mossop* (1988) *The Times* 3 March
6. *Goodman* v *Gallant* (1985) *The Times* 7 November
7. *Pettit* v *Pettit* (1969) 1 All ER 385
8. *Mitchell* v *Mitchell* (1983) *The Times* 6 December

Chapter 2

Legal Procedures, Courts, the Grounds for Divorce and the Undefended Divorce

Who deals with what problems?

The Child Support Agency

All questions involving regular payments for the maintenance of children (it makes no difference if their parents ever married) are now first dealt with by the Child Support Agency set up under the Child Support Act 1991. The Agency will supply details and application forms if you write to it at PO Box 55, Brierley Hill, West Midlands DY5 1YL – or telephone 01345 133133. Chapter 3 covers the way the Agency works.

Magistrates courts

All local magistrates courts include a specialised Family Proceedings Court. Family cases are dealt with in private and cannot be reported.
Family Proceedings Courts deal with the following types of case:

1. Married adults' applications for separation and maintenance orders and for lump sum payments up to £1,000 maximum.
2. Any application for residence, contact, parental responsibility, specific issues, prohibited steps, adoption or lump sum payment (maximum £1,000) order in respect of or for a child.
3. Mothers' applications to decide the paternity of children.
4. Any application for protection against domestic violence by people who live together, married or not.
5. Applications by people under the age of 18 for permission to marry.

The courts now decide which court is best for children's cases. So it no longer matters in which court such cases start. A Family

Proceedings Court may transfer difficult child cases up to a higher court, and higher courts may transfer appropriate ones down to Family Proceedings Courts.

But Family Proceedings Courts have no power to hear divorce or nullity cases which may end marriages; to grant formal decrees of judicial separation; or to make the maintenance and property orders which usually accompany them. So if you want all or any of these you have to go to a higher court, and will then usually also include in such application associated matters (eg involving children) which a Family Proceedings Court could deal with.

Most appeals on family matters from the magistrates go to the Family Division of the High Court.

The County Courts

The County Courts can also deal with all the types of family case which may come before magistrates except paternity cases. In addition, they deal with divorce and nullity cases and with the whole range of money and property issues to which they give rise. All County Court proceedings can be started through your local County Court office. If that office is not itself the office of a Divorce County Court, it will be a sub-branch of one and will be able to issue court proceedings in the name of the appropriate court.

All cases which involve divorce, nullity of marriage and formal applications for decree of judicial separation start with a *petition* (the word used for a summons in these matters) in a Divorce County Court, or in the corresponding office of the principal Divorce Registry in Central London. All are assumed to be undefended, unless, after the petition is issued and served, the other spouse indicates that he or she intends to defend the proceedings. For reasons we shall come to when discussing the basis and procedures for divorce, less than 1 per cent of divorce cases are now defended. If a case raises complicated issues a County Court may transfer it up to the Family Division of the High Court. But the County Courts now deal with the vast majority.

The County Courts have two types of official who may sit as judge in family law cases. Again, the principal Divorce Registry in London has their equivalent. Much County Court work is dealt with by the Court Registrar who is a qualified lawyer. He deals with uncontested adoption cases, all procedural matters, and the large proportion of cases which involve property and money – maintenance, property transfer, lump sum payments and costs. Appeals from the Registrar's decisions on procedural and costs matters go first to the County Court judge. Appeals on property and money matters other than costs go to the Court of Appeal.

The County Court judge pronounces the formal decree nisi of divorce or nullity in open court. Only what he says can be reported. As undefended proceedings are dealt with as a paperwork exercise, this is usually confined to the names and addresses of the parties and the basis on which decree has been granted.

The judge also deals with cases involving the basic arrangements for any children – residence and contact.

The County Court judge may also hear property and money cases, if they are complicated. Any appeal from the County Court judge goes to the Court of Appeal.

The Family Division of the High Court

The Family Division deals with any divorce, children's or financial cases referred up to it by Family Proceedings (magistrates) or County Courts, appeals from Family Proceedings Courts and original applications to make a child a ward of court. Appeals from the Family Division go to the Court of Appeal.

The Court of Appeal and the House of Lords

These courts are only concerned with appeals from lower courts. No case starts in them. Where the Court of Appeal or House of Lords gives leave to appeal, appeals from the Court of Appeal go to the House of Lords. Its decisions are final and can only be overruled by Act of Parliament.

Which do you choose?

Any question of child maintenance must first go to the Child Support Agency. On any other aspect of children's welfare the court itself will decide the level at which it needs to be considered. So it makes no difference where proceedings begin. If you are dealing with your case yourself the magistrates' Family Proceedings Court is likely to prove the easiest in which to start.

If your case involves the ending of your marriage – by divorce or decree of nullity, a formal decree of judicial separation or transfers of property or lump sums of money in excess of the magistrates' £1,000 limit – you have to start in the County Court. If you are not married but your case involves property or savings of any sort, you have to start in the County or High Courts.

If you are married and merely want a temporary separation order, usually with maintenance, you have to start in the magistrates court. You should bear in mind, however, that while magistrates can grant separation orders to the married, there is little point in applying for them if you are already separated.

If you are married and want maintenance from your spouse, or, married or unmarried, want to deal with questions of protection from domestic violence, you can start either in the Family Proceedings or County Courts.

If you wish to take proceedings for the wardship of a child, those proceedings have to be started in the Family Division of the High Court.

The magistrates courts are likely to offer you the cheapest, simplest and often the quickest procedures, particularly if you have agreed everything and all you require is a court order embodying what you have agreed.

Cases in the magistrates court are started by issuing an *application, summons* or *complaint* through your local Justices Clerks office. It is usually easier for people without legal representation to deal with cases in the magistrates court since the subsequent procedure is simpler and the legally qualified magistrates clerk is likely to take a more active role in assisting you when your case comes to court.

But if your financial affairs are complicated, or involve substantial financial sums and problems, the magistrates and their clerk are unlikely to be as well equipped to cope with what is involved as the Registrars and judges in the County Court.

If you decide or have to take your case to the County or High Court, you will find that the initial *application, writ, summons* or *petition* is more complicated than a magistrates court summons and is followed by a series of formal and more complicated procedures laid down by the court rules.

Whether your case begins in the County or High Court, you will usually deal merely with different individuals in the same office initially. In many districts the procedural functions of the County Court and High Court are carried out from the same office and the County Court Registrar is often also the local High Court Registrar. So the chances are that there will only be an apparent physical difference if or when you actually appear in court and find yourself before a County Court or High Court judge. And they may use the same court rooms.

When, why and how do court orders matter?

No capital or property transaction between married people is final and binding unless made, or approved, by a County or High Court order at the conclusion of divorce, nullity or judicial separation proceedings. Anything done before that – which includes marriage contracts and settlements, agreements or transfers of property between you and your partner, and separation agreements or deeds – can be unscrambled and rearranged by the court, so you must obtain such orders if you are to be able to rely on arrangements made. Moreover, such orders must define precisely what your future rights and liabilities are. It is essential that careful thought goes into the words used in them, and that all contingencies are covered.[1] This is particularly so if they operate far ahead in the future – as happens, for example, when wife and children are to stay in the home until the children leave school and the husband is only to receive his share in the home then.

What are the court procedures?

Magistrates court

Family Proceedings cases are started by issuing an application on forms available from the local Justices Clerks general office. Basically, a person must be resident in the area covered by that court to be able to start proceedings in it.

A married person may apply for maintenance, with or without a separation order as circumstances require, if their spouse has:

(a) failed to provide reasonable maintenance, or
(b) behaved in such a way that they cannot reasonably be expected to live with them, or
(c) deserted them.

The application can be made while the couple are still living together, but an order made on the application will not take effect until they separate, and it will cease to operate if they continue to live together for more than six months after it is made.

If the application involves an agreed issue, it will still have to state the basic grounds upon which it is based. In agreed cases the agreement will be spelled out in the application with an application for an order to give effect to the agreement by consent and the order will then be made automatically.

If the application does not relate to an agreed issue, it will merely define the general order required – parental rights, residence, contact with defined children, maintenance for a spouse and so on.

The court will serve the application on the other person or persons involved. The application will state the date, time and place where the case will be considered. A person who is served with an application in family proceedings, or his solicitor, may write for further information before the hearing and may apply for the hearing to be delayed if that information is not forthcoming. But basically there are no formal procedures which intervene between the issue of the application and the hearing.

When the date for the hearing arrives those involved attend court and may give evidence verbally about their case and cross-question those who give evidence against them. The magistrates then make up their minds about what they have heard and reach their decision, which becomes their order.

Unmarried people may only take family cases involving domestic violence or children before the magistrates but the procedures are essentially the same.

If a person is receiving Income Support or Family Support from the Department of Social Security (DSS), the DSS may also apply to the magistrates for maintenance against any spouse or former spouse. It may do that in its own right and whether or not the adults involved wish it. The DSS cannot step in where adults are concerned if there has previously been a final settlement of all their financial affairs under court order at the end of divorce proceedings. But no such settlement affects the powers of the Child Support Agency with regard to children.

County Court

All cases in family matters are started by some form of application, petition or writ. But different, if essentially similar, procedures apply to different types of application. And each type of case – divorce, nullity and so on – has differing qualifying conditions. Divorce is far and away the commonest framework for family proceedings in the

County Court so undefended divorce procedure will serve to illustrate the general pattern. Nullity is now very rare, so this chapter concludes with a brief note on that and other types of family proceedings available in the County Court.

Divorce

(a) The qualifying conditions for divorce

The law lays down qualifying rules that must be satisfied before anyone may issue divorce proceedings. These are:

1. The spouses must have been married for at least 12 months.
2. They must either have their permanent home in England or Wales, or the spouse who wishes to take divorce proceedings (the Petitioner) must have lived in England or Wales for at least 12 months before starting proceedings.
3. The Petitioner must have legal grounds for divorce.
4. Arrangements must have been made for any children of the family.

The grounds for divorce require further explanation.

When parliament reformed divorce law in 1969 it enacted that divorce should only be allowed where a marriage had irretrievably broken down. So, in defining the grounds for divorce, every divorce petition starts with an allegation that this has happened. However, because it was thought to be extremely difficult to be precise when judging what irretrievable breakdown meant, the law went on to define five facts, one or more of which are, if proved by the Petitioner, to be taken as establishing irretrievable breakdown.

These, with their common shorthand versions in parenthesis, are that:

1. The other spouse (the Respondent) has committed adultery *and* the Petitioner finds it intolerable that they continue to live together (*adultery*), or
2. The Respondent has behaved in such a way that the parties cannot reasonably be expected to go on living together (*unreasonable behaviour*), or
3. The Respondent has deserted the Petitioner for a continuous period of two years or more (*desertion*), or
4. The Petitioner and the Respondent have lived apart for a continuous period of at least two years and the Respondent agrees to divorce (*two years' separation by consent*), or

5. The Petitioner and the Respondent have lived apart for a continuous period of at least five years (*five years' separation*).

For the moment the 1969 system rolls on (though adultery petitions do not have to name co-respondents any more). However, major reforms proposed by the Law Commission are summarised in Appendix 4.

Only petitions alleging adultery and unreasonable behaviour can go ahead without any prior period of separation. Around four-fifths of all divorce petitions use these grounds – people usually do not want to hang around once they have decided to divorce. Five years' separation mainly served those who had lived in separated limbo for years before 1969 because they could not prove any ground for divorce under the old law. It is rarely used now.

Unreasonable behaviour is far and away the easiest and most common ground for divorce.

Why is that?

First of all, the law does not define any specific action which amounts to unreasonable behaviour. This distinguishes it immediately from adultery, desertion for two years, or separation for two or five years, which require proof of a specific event. Moreover, the test for unreasonable behaviour allows wide margins for subjective views: it is, in the words used in a 1987 case, 'not whether the behaviour has been of a grave and weighty nature but whether a right-thinking person, knowing the parties and all the circumstances, would consider it unreasonable to expect the Petitioner to live with the Respondent'.[2]

So what tends to happen in practice is that Petitioners think back through the history of their marriages and list in petitions all the things which have happened which they consider unreasonable. Since memories are always selective, and often exclude the circumstances which prompted events, though the events themselves are clear, virtually anyone who has been married for any period of time can produce a list of behaviour which appears sufficiently unreasonable to convince a right-thinking person.

That unreasonable behaviour might not seem so unreasonable if one added the Respondent's version of the same events and many Respondents, when they receive such petitions, are wholly unconvinced. Indeed, if they were right-thinking persons before they received their petitions, they cease to be so afterwards – unless a draft of the terms of the petition has already been made known to them beforehand and has been tacitly agreed to facilitate a swift and harmonious divorce.

But suppose it has not been agreed? Will they not then defend the case and reveal the whole picture?

At this stage procedural and cost rules are usually decisive. Respondents often want to put the record straight. They want to fight the case and consult a solicitor for advice about defending it. They are told that it is against their interests to do so. They are told that what is said in the petition will almost certainly have no bearing at all on future decisions about things which matter – money, property and children. They are further told that if they fight, the only consequence will be to create great delay, and to achieve a tenfold or more increase in the costs of the divorce on its own – which they may have to pay. Undefended divorce has become a purely paperwork exercise. But a defended divorce includes all the procedures, paperwork and evidence of a trial. And the divorce costs are additional to those which will arise from any disputes over children and money, which are likely to be the same whatever happens to the divorce.

Taken aback, Respondents may grasp at the last straw – legal aid. If they have limited means they might qualify – on the means test. That may encourage them to think that they can still put up a fight when having to pay costs to their solicitor immediately would itself persuade them otherwise. So they apply for legal aid. But it is now general policy that legal aid is not available to cover the divorce proceedings themselves and is not granted to defend them. Legal aid is therefore refused.

So the law has become a fiction. Respondents do not defend. Their version of the unreasonable behaviour never sees the light of day and they succumb, often angrily, to a reality which the law does not spell out – if a Petitioner has issued a divorce petition which clearly evidences that he or she is hell-bent on divorce, no practical purpose is served by allowing anyone to fight over it.

This is why the large majority of divorce petitions allege unreasonable behaviour; why over 99 per cent of all divorces now go through undefended; why reform is now likely; and why it is needed.

(b) The procedure on undefended divorce

The Petitioner, who is initiating the action, must first prepare his or her petition. Different printed blank forms are available from law stationers and from most County Court offices for each of the five different bases for divorce. Notes printed on the forms will guide you when filling them in. A Petitioner may not obtain legal aid for the divorce itself – only for the so-called ancillary matters dealing with property, money and children. But either party who qualifies on financial grounds may obtain legal advice and guidance on the petition from a solicitor under the Green Form Legal Advice Scheme which any solicitor can explain and which is discussed in greater detail in Chapter 11.

The Petitioner has to fill in all the details required by the form. These include:

(a) the full names of husband and wife
(b) the full names and dates of birth of any children under 18
(c) full details of the date and place of marriage as shown on the marriage certificate
(d) details of any previous matrimonial proceedings
(e) details of the chosen ground or grounds for divorce
(f) details of ancillary orders sought to deal with money matters and any children.

If there are children – and these include children who have been accepted as members of the family as well as children natural-born to the Petitioner and Respondent – the Petitioner also has to complete a separate form detailing the arrangements proposed for the children.

If the petition is based on five years' separation and Petitioner and Respondent have discussed divorce and all its implications, the petition must set out anything which they have been able to agree. But otherwise matters involving property and money will only be dealt with at or after decree nisi (explained on page 31).

When the documents are complete, with or without prior discussion or agreement, the Petitioner issues the petition by sending the following to his or her local divorce County Court office:

1. The petition, together with a spare copy for service.
2. If there are children, a standard form statement of the arrangements for them – also in duplicate.
3. The marriage certificate. A copy can be obtained from the Registrar General[3] if the original is not available.
4. The fee of £40 payable on the issue of the petition. (People on Income or Family Support and those qualifying for advice under the Green Form Scheme can claim exemption from this fee.)

In a minority of cases a Petitioner may need to apply for provisional but immediate help – maintenance or exclusion of a spouse from the home, for example – as soon as proceedings start and in anticipation of final decisions on these matters after the divorce itself is complete. (Such interim assistance is covered briefly and simply in the sections below dealing with money and property.)

If the Petitioner has asked a solicitor to act for him or her, the solicitor will deal with all these matters. He will also advise about legal aid applications for the things for which legal aid is available.

Once received, the documents will be checked by the County Court to see that they are in order. Provided they are, it will then post a copy of the petition and of any statement of children's arrangements to the other spouse – the Respondent. With them will go a form for *acknowledgement of service* which the Respondent is required to complete and return to the court within 14 days. The Respondent has to indicate in the acknowledgement of service whether or not he or she intends to defend the petition or any of the claims in it and the case cannot go ahead until the court has proof that the petition has been served. If the Respondent fails to return the acknowledgement, the Petitioner may arrange for further copies to be served personally – typically by an enquiry agent. Personal service immediately adds to the costs of the divorce which the Respondent may have to pay, so Respondents should not hang back from returning the acknowledgement. But they should take advice from a solicitor before sending the acknowledgement back if they do not fully understand what it is all about.

If the Respondent indicates in the acknowledgement that he or she intends to defend the divorce, the Respondent must then file an answer to the divorce – ie a defence – which may also contain a cross-petition. In simple words, this is a way of saying that the Respondent denies that the Petitioner is entitled to a divorce, for reasons which are given; and, if there is a cross-petition, that the Respondent considers that he or she is entitled to divorce the Petitioner on one of the five grounds which must also be defined.

As already indicated, defending a divorce adds massively to delay and costs. Defending may offer a tactical advantage if the Petitioner is in a great hurry to achieve a divorce; and that advantage may then be realised by negotiation so that the case can then proceed to an undefended conclusion on agreed terms. But defended cases are so rare, and their complications so much greater, that no one should consider launching themselves into a defended case without full legal advice from a solicitor. And since the solicitor will probably then conduct the proceedings, we will limit discussion of defended proceedings to that.

When the Respondent returns the acknowledgement of service to the court, the court will send a copy to the Petitioner. If the acknowledgement indicates that the Respondent does not intend to defend, the Petitioner may then apply to the Court for directions for trial. This involves completing and sending to the Registrar at the County Court two more forms – also available from law stationers and divorce County Courts:

1. An affidavit declaring the truth of the allegations in the petition to which is attached any evidence supporting the allegations in the petition – eg enquiry agents' reports, medical reports or signed confessions of adultery.
2. An application for directions which defines the details to be dealt with when the judge considers the papers.

An *affidavit* is a formal written statement sworn on oath before a solicitor (who will charge a fee) or before a County Court officer (who will not charge).

The Court Registrar will then consider the forms and, if they are in order, will give directions for trial. The court will then send to both Petitioner and Respondent a notice detailing when and where the judge will sit to consider granting the decree nisi of divorce. If children are involved, that notice will also give details of the separate appointment for the children.

If no one appears to object to the decree nisi (see page 31) it will then be granted automatically. No one need attend the court hearing unless they wish to object. But if there are children, and unless the court previously indicates that it will accept evidence on affidavit, the parent seeking a residence order for the children must attend on the children's appointment, and it is often desirable for both parents to be present.

(c) The children

The children's appointment is held in private, in judges' chambers. It is entirely informal and unless the parents still dispute any matter relating to the children, neither of them need be legally represented. They do not have to be in any case but legal representation is wise if there is a dispute. If everything is agreed, the judge may ask a few questions about the children and their welfare and if all then seems well, he will express himself:

(a) satisfied with the arrangements proposed for the children, or
(b) satisfied that the arrangements are the best available in the circumstances.

He will then make the formal orders relating to the children as requested in the proceedings.

The court will then send both spouses a copy of the formal order making the decree nisi and the children's orders. This will include orders relating to the welfare of the children. In the standard form it will include in particular orders that the children shall not be taken out of the country or have their names changed without the consent of the other parent, or the court. Once parents have brought any proceedings to court which relate to children, the court has the last say on matters which affect those children until they are 18.

If there is any dispute about the children, or if for any reason the judge is not satisfied with the arrangements proposed for them, he will adjourn the case, possibly for a full court hearing if disputes cannot otherwise be resolved. A few judges ask for court child welfare officers' reports to assist them in all children's cases. But the large majority only ask for such reports if there is a dispute or if problems emerge at the children's appointment.

So far as the divorce itself is concerned, however, although the decree nisi has been pronounced it cannot be made absolute until the judge has expressed himself satisfied in one or other of the alternative forms. In addition, in cases where the parties are still living together under the same roof, the court may direct that the decree absolute shall not be granted until they have actually separated. So what is the distinction between the two decrees?

(d) Decree nisi and decree absolute

Decree nisi is a provisional decree of divorce only – a decree unless cause is later shown why it should not take effect. It does not end the marriage, nor does it alter the fact that husband and wife are still legally husband and wife and are still, for example, guilty of bigamy if they remarry. Only the decree absolute ends the marriage.

If no conditions are attached to making the decree nisi absolute and unless late objections are raised, decree absolute is then a formality. Once six weeks have passed from the date of the decree nisi, the Petitioner may apply to have the decree made absolute – another standard form and another fee, this time £15. If the Petitioner fails to apply, the Respondent may apply once three months have passed from the date of decree nisi. However, if neither party applies for some months, the Court Registrar may require additional information, usually by affidavit, to explain the delay and to satisfy the court in particular that the parties have not started living together again as man and wife in the meantime.

(e) Costs of the divorce alone

The orders made by the court may also include orders as to costs if the Petitioner has asked for costs, or the parties have agreed a specific costs order. A court may or may not order the Respondent to pay all or some part of the costs: it does not have to.

Costs orders, particularly on undefended divorce alone, are increasingly uncommon. They occur more frequently at the conclusion of subsequent proceedings dealing with children, money and property. In any event, costs are dealt with when everything else is completed so we will deal with the costs procedures at the conclusion of this account (see pages 35–6).

(f) How long does it take?

From what has been said it will be seen that obtaining a divorce and dealing with children's issues is largely a paperwork formality in undisputed cases. No more than three or four months need elapse from start to finish if everyone deals with the paperwork as swiftly as possible. But if they do not, or if there are disputes over maintenance or property, cases can drag on for years.

(g) Property and money

Interim measures

Although final orders on property and money can only be made after decree nisi, it is sometimes necessary to obtain interim protection before or while divorce proceedings are running. A spouse may have no income to live on, may be under great pressure if both continue to live under the same roof, or may need to stop his or her partner from making off with family property before a court can make any final orders on it.

Weekly or monthly *maintenance* for spouses can, in appropriate circumstances, be claimed at any time during a marriage in the magistrates or County Courts, and without any question of divorce arising. In addition, a Petitioner (or Respondent) who does not have adequate income to keep him or her going can apply for interim maintenance as soon as divorce proceedings are started. Applications can also be made during the proceedings for injunctions to prevent a spouse from *dissipating assets* belonging to either of the parties and to exclude (oust) a spouse on a provisional basis from the matrimonial home. However, *ouster orders* will not be made merely to save people the embarrassment of continuing to live under the same roof while one of them is divorcing the other. The courts have said that an ouster order 'requiring the husband to leave the matrimonial home is a very serious order which should be made only on the judge being satisfied that no lesser measure would be sufficient for the protection of the wife and children'.[4] Effectively, ouster orders will usually only be granted to protect against domestic violence or

something very similar. Where appropriate, however, they ma
granted against wives as well as husbands.

Final measures

The court will not accept any application for permanent maintenance,
or any application to confirm the ownership of or to redistribute
property by property transfer or lump sum order, until the decree nisi
has been granted. If an order is made for permanent maintenance,
however, that does not mean the amount is permanent. It may be
varied in future.

A basic caution

The fact that money questions can only be dealt with after decree nisi,
and decree absolute – and then remarriage – may follow soon after,
brings with it the need for a particular warning. A spouse's right to
maintenance ends automatically if that spouse remarries. But
remarriage also ends the right even to apply for a property order
unless the application has been made before the remarriage. So if you
intend to remarry as soon as you are free to do so, remember that if
you wish to apply for an order involving property, the application
must go into the court before the remarriage. Even if you have not
obtained a solicitor's advice on anything else, you should take such
advice if you plan to remarry before everything has been sorted out.

Procedures on property and money

In the ideal case, Petitioner and Respondent, on their own or through
negotiations between their solicitors, will agree all the details of their
future financial arrangements before decree nisi. They will decide
what is to happen to the house; whether there is to be a clean break
with no ongoing maintenance; and, even if there is to be a clean break,
what property, if any, is to be retained by or transferred between them.

If there is not to be a clean break, they will agree what continuing
maintenance the husband shall pay to the wife, or, more rarely, the
wife to the husband. They will agree if there is to be any extra
provision for children on top of that which the Child Support Agency
will assess – for example, by payment of school fees. In some cases
they may agree to transfer property to the children, or to trustees who
will hold it for the children. They will agree what is to happen about
costs.

If everything is agreed and then embodied in a summons detailing
all the agreements, the Petitioner and Respondent can apply for a

consent order to give legal effect to that agreement immediately after decree nisi.

To do that they will need to send to the court:

1. The summons detailing all the arrangements in a form which the court can follow in making formal orders. This summons must be signed by the parties to indicate their consent or by their solicitors on their behalf.
2. The statement of information for a consent order (a standard form laid down by the Matrimonial Causes Rules (MCR)). Details must be given of the financial position – income, cash, property, mortgages and debts – of both parties and whether they intend to remarry or cohabit or are already doing so so that the court can see the background against which the summons is applied for and can satisfy itself that the matters agreed are reasonable.

If the court is satisfied, the Registrar will make the order as requested without anyone needing to attend. The order will then be served on the parties and that will be the end of it.

Unfortunately, this only happens in a minority of cases – usually those where Petitioner and Respondent are sufficiently rich to be able to make reasonable overall provision, or sufficiently wise to realise how much of their joint fortune will be lost in costs if they fight.

Where there is no agreement, either party who seeks financial orders must first serve notice indicating the orders sought in a form laid down by the Matrimonial Causes Rules (MCR), even though the petition will have outlined the financial relief sought by the Petitioner. Anyone who sends such a notice to the court must also send with it an affidavit of their means which must detail their whole financial position – income, capital, savings, debts, liabilities and so on.

The court will then serve a copy of the notice of application on the other party together with a copy of the affidavit. That party in turn must file an affidavit detailing his or her means. There may then follow applications by letter, and failing that to the court, requiring the disclosure of further information and the supply of data (accounts, bank statements and so on), questionnaires about means, cross affidavits and further affidavits dependent on the circumstances – and often on the degree of rancour which separates the parties. Suffice it to say that if spouses feel bloody-minded about each other, their bloody-mindedness is likely to emerge in full splendour at this stage – and at rapidly escalating cost to both of them.

If a negotiated settlement becomes possible while all this is going on, the merry-go-round can then be called to a halt by a consent application to the court. Otherwise the court will eventually fix a date and time for the matter to be heard. In the County Court that will usually be before the Court Registrar, although he may refer a particular case to the judge. The parties can attend the hearing, and frequently do in difficult cases, with or without their lawyers. The Registrar (or judge) will then consider the details disclosed by the affidavits, but verbal evidence may also be accepted.[5] At the conclusion, the Registrar or judge will announce his decisions, and these will be embodied in court orders and served on the parties, with or without orders for costs as the court considers necessary or appropriate. In the absence of appeals the orders take effect, and legal procedures can be used to enforce or attempt to enforce them if they are not complied with voluntarily.

Costs

We are here concerned with the procedures for dealing with costs orders only. The basis for calculating costs is dealt with later in Chapter 11. If either party has been legally aided, there will be an order for the taxation of that party's legal aid costs against the Legal Aid Fund. If either party is ordered to pay the costs of the other, or any part of them, there will usually be an order that those costs be decided by taxation if they cannot be agreed.

So what is taxation?

Taxation of costs

Taxation is a formal process that is started, following an order for costs, when a highly technical and formalised bill covering solicitors' costs, barristers' fees, disbursements and VAT is lodged with the court for a taxation appointment. Most lawyers use specialised law costs draftsmen to prepare these bills. The person entitled to costs has to draw up the bill of costs and deliver it, with defined supporting documents, to the court with copies for service on the person against whom the order is made. Normally it should be delivered within three months of the date of the final costs order, but frequently it is not.

Both parties (or their solicitors) are then given notice of an appointment before the Registrar when he will accept representations from the parties about the individual items, examine the bill in detail and decide exactly how much is allowable and payable. Court rules define some figures allowable on taxation; others depend on the Registrar's discretion exercised in the light of the work which has been done and the degree of skill, responsibility and complexity which it has entailed. The decision of the Registrar or other taxing officer is then a judgment of the court, and, unless appealed, is enforceable against the person liable to the costs, or with legal aid orders, the Legal Aid Fund, like any other judgment for money. But it should be emphasised that neither an order for costs, nor the Registrar's taxation of the specific amount, necessarily means that the party entitled to costs will get anything. Orders for costs are subject to the same hazards as any other judgments for money – if the person liable for the costs does not pay, and has no property or money against which payment can be enforced, it may not be possible to recover the costs.

The amount of costs

Taxation is a private procedure and there is no general public record of how much divorce or any other cases cost. Cost figures only appear in the law reports occasionally when there is an appeal about costs. But two decisions will give the flavour of the problem.

In *Leary* v *Leary*, reported in *The Times* on 7 October 1987, the court ordered a husband to pay a fixed sum of £31,000 costs and that decision was upheld when he took the question to the Court of Appeal – at further cost, of course. In *Clark* v *Clark*, reported in *The Times* on 31 March 1988, the wife obtained legal aid to take proceedings to recover £5,000 arrears of maintenance; £17,000 was recovered from the husband but that was not enough to cover her legal aid costs, never mind the £5,000 she was claiming, so she recovered nothing.

Finally, there was a case in 1982 where the Court of Appeal came up with a view of the law which astonished many people. It seemed likely that it would be reversed if further appealed to the House of Lords and the husband was so advised. But he was also advised that he was already liable for £72,000 costs and, quite simply, he could not afford to take the matter any further. He therefore had to settle.

No husband, wife or cohabitee should be in any doubt that the cost of fighting about income or property may be such that they end up with much less than they expected – sometimes nothing – even if they win.

Other County Court family jurisdictions

We have already noted in passing that County Courts can deal with applications for maintenance and those relating to children apart from any question of divorce, and with adoption and domestic violence cases.

A final note is required on nullity.

Nullity of marriage

Nullity may arise in two cases:

1. Where there was never any legal marriage at all – for example, where one of the parties was still married so that it was bigamous. Here the court may make a declaration of nullity.
2. Where, on the face of it, there was a legal marriage, but some fundamental flaw makes it voidable – where, for example, it has not been consummated.

In either type of nullity case the courts can still make all the orders generally available in respect of any children. In cases where there was never any legal marriage the court can still deal with the property of the parties as if they were cohabitees. In cases where the marriage is voidable the court can still make the same sort of financial orders between the parties as it can in divorce.

Nullity cases are now very rare, not least because the circumstances which may give rise to them are rare and most voidable marriages can also be terminated by divorce proceedings.

Notes

1. *Dinch* v *Dinch* (1987) *The Times* 21 February
2. *Buffery* v *Buffery* (1987) *The Times* 10 December
3. The Registrar of Marriages, St Catherine's House, 10 Kingsway, London WC2B 6JP
4. *Reid* v *Reid* (1984) *The Times* 30 July
5. *Krywald* v *Krywald* (1988) *The Times* 19 March

Chapter 3

The Child Support Agency

Introduction

This chapter is essential reading if you live in the United Kingdom and:

1. You are a parent – father, mother or legal adopter of a child here, or,
2. You have married or are living with such a parent, or,
3. You have care of a child here for such parents.

'Child' includes anyone under the age of 16, and anyone who has not married and is still in full-time education up to the age of 19. Such children are called 'Qualifying Children'.

If you do not fall in any of these categories you may if you wish turn straight to Chapter 4.

The legal framework

The Child Support Act 1991 ('The Act') set up an entirely new system for calculating and collecting maintenance for children ('Child Support'). It established the Child Support Agency ('The Agency') to run that system.

The Act means little on its own. Regulations made after it was passed define the detail of more than a hundred of its provisions. And the mathematical formulae for calculating maintenance (set out in the Act) involve the use of DSS Income Support allowances which anyway change annually.

The Agency publishes detailed guides and instructions to the working of the Act (its introductory guide 'For Parents who live Apart' is available in Post Offices). These give a reasonably clear picture of the practical end results of the Act and of all its subordinate regulations. Anyone concerned about Child Support should therefore obtain and study them. Anyone determined to study the chapter and verse of the Act and its regulations is likely to benefit from first reading them.

Changes to the original rules

The rules which first governed the Agency were modified in February 1994. These changes are built into the text which follows. Then on 20 December 1994 it was announced (government statement) that the Agency would delay taking up any more cases where the Parent with Care of Qualifying Children was receiving means-tested DSS benefits before April 1993; or where the Agency wrote to such a parent before 1 July 1994 and received no effective reply. So if your case is in those categories the Agency will not be doing anything about it unless or until further announcements are made. Finally, (as at 23 January 1995), the White Paper 'Improving Child Support' proposed more radical changes. These will not be effective until implemented by legislation and none of them will affect calculations of child support (or accumulated arrears) for periods before they come into force.

The text which follows therefore states the position as it will exist unless or until the White Paper's proposals are implemented and identifies and notes the intended changes by prefixing them with their *proposed* implementation dates – 'after April 1995' or 'after 1996/7'. If or when your case is referred to the Agency it should be able to confirm the extent to which any of the relevant changes are then in force.

Payment periods

Child Support is calculated on a weekly basis, but if agreed it may be paid monthly or over other periods. It is payable by parents who live apart from their children ('Absent Parents') to those living with them ('Parents with Care').

Transitional arrangements

All new child maintenance cases arising after 5 April 1993 must first go to and through the Agency. The position with cases existing before that date is as follows:

(a) If the Parent with Care of Qualifying Children was receiving DSS means-tested benefits and the Agency had not taken up their case by 20 December 1993, it will not now take their case on unless or until the government decides that the Agency can cope – and maybe never (see above). In the meantime such parents will continue to qualify for DSS benefits as before.

(b) If Parents with Care were not receiving DSS benefits but were receiving child maintenance under a court order or maintenance agreement (and the Agency has not already taken on their case) the courts will continue to deal with their cases, and apply court principles to them (see Chapter 6) – at least until some date after 1996/97. But if in the meantime they are having difficulty in collecting that maintenance it is hoped (White Paper) that it will become possible for the Agency to take on the job of enforcing payment – subject to the payment of the current Agency collection fees (see below page 46).

(c) Where the Agency has already taken on cases existing before April 1993:

 • The courts can revoke or cancel any pre-existing court order or maintenance agreement – so that the parent liable to pay (the Absent Parent) does not face a double liability.

 • If Child Support exceeds £60 a week, Absent Parents with new families who have been paying child maintenance under previous arrangements only pay the full amount of any *increase* after two years. These are the intervening stages:

1. *First six months* – Existing payment plus a quarter of the extra or £20, whichever is more.
2. *Second six months* – Existing payment plus half the extra or £40, whichever is more.
3. *Third six months* – Existing payment plus three quarters the extra, or £60, whichever is more.
4. Thereafter the full amount.

Child Support and court financial powers compared

The courts start with the facts – the parties' net financial resources. They arrive at their answers – financial provision orders – by judging how general principles defined in law (see further Chapter 4) apply to the facts. In that exercise they use a handful of specific rules of thumb which they have found consistent with the general principles over the years, and these certainly could be systematised – as Chapter 6 illustrates for maintenance; and as Scottish law has for property (see Chapter 7, pages 102–4).

The Agency starts with the answers it must aim for – a basic target for maintenance made up of defined DSS allowances, plus, where means allow, a defined percentage of the Absent Parent's income, which is fixed without reference to the relationship between the Absent Parent's and Parent with Care's income. Then it considers, subject to defined rules, the extent to which the facts make it possible to achieve the answers. Thus the court approach is essentially a scientific approach – proceeding from facts to answers – and the Agency's is not. This may explain why the Agency has already produced bizarre results.

It is still only the courts which can:

(a) order one party to a marriage to pay maintenance to the other ('Adult Maintenance')

(b) make lump sum, property transfer and other property orders between spouses or former spouses

(c) order one party to a marriage to pay maintenance for a child of whom that party is not father or mother, eg a step-child accepted as a child of the family

(d) make lump sum, property transfer and other property orders in favour of children – who may qualify for such orders whether or not their parents were married (see further Chapters 4–7).

Only where parental circumstances allow can the courts now order a father or mother to pay general child maintenance additional to Child Support – and then only after Child Support has first been assessed. But the courts can make special maintenance orders for or towards the cost of educating a child or supporting a disabled child.[1] Because of the levels of Child Support such orders are unlikely unless parents are seriously rich (see below, pages 53–4).

But Child Support, if payable, now affects all the powers which the courts retain. Before making any financial decision in family matters courts must first have regard to the parties' overall position. Child Support radically affects those positions because:

(a) the right to claim, or liability to pay, Child Support continues until all Qualifying Children come of age, and

(b) the courts have no power to alter or amend the amount of Child Support, or to exclude or restrict the right to claim it or the liability to pay. And parents cannot make any legally enforceable agreement to do any of these things.

So no one can now look sensibly at any question of other financial provision in families with Qualifying Children until the impact of Child Support has been assessed and the parents' respective financial positions have been adjusted to take account of it – by deducting the amount of Child Support from the income of the Absent Parent and adding it to the income of the Parent with Care.

But Child Support may additionally affect the value of a parent's capital and savings. Child Support is payable from the time the agency sends out its form requiring details of means to the absent parent or (after April 1995) eight weeks after that date if the absent parent replies within four weeks. The starting date – whatever it may be – is likely to be some time before the amount payable is assessed, and the amount assessed may be substantially more than has been paid in the meantime. So a calculation of arrears (after April 1995 these may be limited to six months but only if the Absent Parent otherwise performs *all* his or her obligations) may well accompany the assessment when it is made. Any debt for arrears will reduce the capital, savings or other property of the Absent Parent, increase the savings of the Parent with Care, and require capital adjustments as well.

Under the general law applied in the courts an adult may only be ordered to maintain another adult if:

(a) they are or have been married, and
(b) there has been no clean break settlement approved by a court following divorce proceedings (see further Chapter 8), and
(c) the adult claiming maintenance has not remarried.

The Act has driven a coach and horses through these principles. The formulae for calculating Child Support include substantial provision for the Parent with Care – effectively maintenance for that parent (see below, pages 47–8). And Child Support is payable as long as children qualify, regardless of the parents' status. So Absent Parents paying Child Support must now also support Parents with Care regardless of whether such parents have remarried or were ever married; and regardless of any clean break settlement.

Any property transfer or clean break settlement made after April 1993 should have taken account of Child Support (see Chapter 5, page 78) and will be assumed to have done so. Some relief is now proposed for transfers made before that date:

(a) After April 1995 Absent Parents will be able to claim a broad-brush allowance if they can prove that, valued as at the date of transfer, half the net value of anything transferred to the Parent with Care exceeded £5,000. Why half? The Parent with Care is assumed to have been entitled to half anyway. The allowance is likely to come by way of a weekly deduction from the formula calculation of Child Support – the amount depending on whether the transfer falls in the £5,000–£9,999, £10,000–£25,000, or above £25,000 bands. As an example only, the White Paper suggests weekly deductions of £20, £40 and £60 for the three bands.

(b) After 1996/97 either parent may apply for further discretionary review of any such allowance on the basis that it is too generous or is not generous enough (see 'Discretionary appeals', pages 54–5).

But unless there has been such a transfer the position of unmarried and remarried parents will stay as it is.

The courts have to consider the 'net effect' of financial decisions on the parties before exercising their powers (see also Chapter 5, pages 70–1). To do that they take into account – in each case – the whole range of the parties' actual income, assets and commitments so as to ensure that they only order a person to pay real money – money which he or she actually has available; and only allow a person to receive money which he or she actually needs.

Superficially the rules under which the Agency operates include similar provisions. But they are more restrictive.

For example, when considering the income out of which a person may reasonably be ordered to pay maintenance, the courts are likely to allow deduction of the full amount of any pension or superannuation contributions which he or she has to make. The Agency's rules only allow deduction of half of those payments. Again a court is likely to allow the deduction of a party's reasonable costs of travelling to work and full housing costs, even if he or she has a new partner (with or without children), unless that partner (or those children) also have significant income. But the Agency's original rules stipulated *automatic* reductions in housing costs in any case where a parent liable to pay Child Support was living with a new partner and any step-children, and gave no allowance for travel. Only after April 1995 will the Agency's rules allow for 'high' travel costs and housing costs regardless of second families (see 'Assessable income', page 51).

Because of enduring differences the Agency is still likely to assess Child Support on figures which assume that parents have more income available than courts would assume for court maintenance. And the higher the parents' incomes the greater the difference is likely to be.

For more than 20 years the courts have generally (but not

universally) taken the view that a person living on DSS Income Support or other means tested allowance should only be ordered to pay nominal maintenance – 5p a year, for example. The reason has been that these DSS allowances are designed to cover bare subsistence and leave no margin out of which they can reasonably be ordered to maintain someone else (see also Chapter 6, pages 96–7).

The Act has rejected that view. Unless disabled, a person living on Income Support must surrender 5 per cent of that income towards Child Support.

The courts have always applied an overriding upper limit to the amount of maintenance, however they might calculate it. The object of maintenance has always been seen as *compensating* the *maintained person* for the financial support lost as the result of family breakdown – as far as the divided resources of the parties allow. It has not been to make people better off (see also Chapter 6, pages 97–8). So courts are not likely to order maintenance which exceeds that sufficient to allow the maintained individual to continue the standard of living which the parties' means allowed, or would have allowed, while they were together.

Child Support is not subject to any comparable upper limit. The amount of Child Support payable is anyway likely to exceed that required to preserve the relevant child's standard of living – if only because Child Support includes provision for the Parent with Care. And the higher the income of the Absent Parent, the greater *that* excess is likely to be. Moreover, at the opposite end of the scale, if an Absent Parent has income capable of assessment by the Agency some Child Support will be payable even if the Parent with Care is substantially better off; even if the Parent with Care's own means are more than sufficient to sustain that parent and family; and even in circumstances in which a court might order the Parent with Care to pay maintenance to and for the Absent Parent (see also Chapter 6, Case 5, page 92).

Court decisions can be appealed through the established court hierarchy – if need be to the House of Lords (see further Chapter 2). There is no appeal into the ordinary courts against decision of the Agency.

The Agency's initial maintenance assessments are made by one of its Child Support Officers. A person dissatisfied with such an assessment may ask for it to be reviewed by another officer; and may appeal to the independent Child Support Appeal Tribunal set up under the Act if still not satisfied. But that is the end of the defined rights of appeal. And such an appeal is only likely to succeed if it can be shown that the rules have been incorrectly applied. The fact that the rules may have produced bizarre results is not a ground of appeal.

However, after 1996/97 either parent may ask for a discretionary adjustment of Child Support to allow for exceptional expenses, debts jointly incurred before separation, or property settlements made before April 1993 (see 'Discretionary appeals', pages 54–5).

The mechanics of Child Support

Who applies?

If you have Qualifying Children living with you – normally they will be your own, but other relatives with their care may also apply – you may, as Parent with Care, apply to have Child Support assessed against their Absent Parent.

If you are receiving DSS social security benefits – Income Support, Family Credit or Disability Working Allowance – you *must* apply; and you must then cooperate with the Agency in pursuing the application, or risk losing a significant part of your DSS benefits. You are only spared that risk if you can satisfy the Agency that you or any child living with you may suffer harm or undue distress if the Agency takes action on your behalf.[2]

If you are an Absent Parent of Qualifying Children you also may apply for a Child Support assessment with regard to them. You might think that you are inviting unnecessary trouble if you do. But you also need to know what your future Child Support liabilities are; and you may face additional problems if the Parent with Care is slow off the mark and an assessment is not available when you or your advisers need it. Bear in mind the point made above, under the heading 'Child Support and court financial powers compared', pages 41–2.

How do you apply?

Ask the Agency (PO Box 55, Brierley Hill, West Midlands DY5 1YL; 01345 133133) for the forms and information leaflets appropriate to your case. The application form is 36 pages long, and requires a vast amount of detail. You will receive detailed instruction notes from the Agency to guide you, but if you still need help a solicitor, an accountant or the Citizens' Advice Bureau may be able to help you.

Complete the form and return it to the Agency as soon as possible.

What fees are payable?

(a) If the Agency is empowered to collect maintenance due under agreements or court orders made before April 1993 (see page 40 above) parents who apply for that service will pay the annual Agency collection fee (currently £34).

(b) After April 1995 and until April 1997 all other fees are suspended.

(c) Subject to that no fees are payable anyway if you have to make an application because you are receiving Income Support, Family Credit or Disability Working Allowance, or are an Absent Parent receiving any of those benefits or are under 16 years of age.

Otherwise (at current rates):

1. As a Parent with Care you will pay £44 if you only want the Agency to *assess* the amount of Child Support; £78 if you want the Agency both to *assess* the amount and then also to *collect* it on your behalf. These fees (or any substituted for them) are then payable annually until Child Support ceases to be due – the Agency reviews and, if appropriate, adjusts assessments on evidence of a change in the circumstances of either parent and otherwise (after April 1995) every two years.

2. Absent Parents pay the same fees as Parents with Care in addition to any payable by those parents. Absent Parents who are not exempt (see above) still pay if the Parent with Care is exempt.

What happens when the Agency has received the application?

If the other parent's address is not known the Agency will attempt to trace him or her – it has access to National Insurance and Inland Revenue records for that purpose, something which courts and parents have never had.

Once the other parent's address is known the Agency will send an equally detailed form to that parent requiring full details of his or her position.

The liability to pay any Child Support eventually assessed runs from the date when the Agency sends that form out to the other parent – or (after April 1995) eight weeks after that date if the Absent Parent completes and returns his (or her) form within four weeks.

If the other parent does not complete and return the form, the Agency will assess Child Support on the basis of the information it has already received and will issue an interim (provisional) assessment. Any interim assessment is likely to be pitched at levels which require significantly more Child Support than would probably be due if the Agency had received full information – the same technique the Inland Revenue uses when people fail to submit tax returns. But (as with Inland Revenue assessments) interim assessments are legally effective; Child Support is payable in accordance with them until such time as the Agency receives sufficient information to prompt any revision.

If you receive a form requesting information from the Agency do not drag your feet before completing and returning it.

How is Child Support calculated and assessed?

The overall picture

The basic objective of the Act is to ensure that, wherever possible, Parents with Care do not end up relying on DSS Income Support for maintenance. So the basic target figure for Child Support – the Maintenance Requirement – is calculated by working out how much DSS Income Support Parents with Care would be entitled to if they received no maintenance from the Absent Parent and had no income of their own.

The question of whether that target can actually be met depends on the Assessable Incomes of both parents. Assessable Income is what is left after defined financial liabilities and expenses have been subtracted from the parents' total gross incomes.

If a Parent with Care has no Assessable Income and the Absent Parent's Assessable Income is not more than twice the Maintenance Requirement, the Child Support payable by the Absent Parent will be half his (or her) Assessable Income. If the Absent Parent's Assessable Income is greater than twice the Maintenance Requirement, the Child Support will be:

(a) The amount of the Maintenance Requirement, plus
(b) Fifteen per cent of the amount by which Assessable Income exceeds twice the Maintenance Requirement if there is one child; 20 per cent for two children; and 25 per cent for three or more.

Thus Child Support absorbs half an Absent Parent's Assessable Income up to the point where the Maintenance Requirement is covered; and after that 15 per cent, 20 per cent or 25 per cent depending on the number of Qualifying Children.

If both parents have Assessable Incomes these are added together. If the total is less than twice the Maintenance Requirement the Child Support payable by the Absent Parent is half his (or her) Assessable Income – as it would be if the Parent with Care had no income. If the total is more than the Maintenance Requirement, the Absent Parent contributes to the Maintenance Requirement in the proportion which his (or her) income bears to that of the Parent with Care. But if there is still assessable income left after the Maintenance Requirement is covered the Absent Parent then pays 15, 20 or 25 per cent (dependent on the number of children) of the excess regardless of the relationship between the means of the parents. The following example may help to make sense of that infernal complexity:

Suppose John's Assessable Income is £150, Anne's is £50 (ie 75 per cent:25 per cent) and the Maintenance Requirement for one child in Anne's care is £80. In such a case the Child Support figures would work out like this:

1. John's 75 per cent of the Maintenance Requirement = £60.
2. He has to devote half his Assessable Income to the basic Maintenance Requirement liability so £120 of his Assessable Income has been used to provide that £60.
3. That leaves £30 of his Assessable Income liable to additional assessment at 15 per cent for one child = £4.50.
4. John's total Child Support assessment would be £64.50.

Anne's contribution is reflected in the fact that Child Support payable is £15.50 less than the Maintenance Requirement; less obviously in the fact that she does not receive, or of course need to receive, 15 per cent on the £10 of her income not taken up to cover her half of that requirement.

But this emphasises another aspect of the percentages fixed for contribution on top of the Maintenance Requirement. Both parents are equally liable to contribute to the support of their children. So in requiring Absent Parents to pay 15 per cent, 20 per cent or 25 per cent of their 'surplus' Assessable Income, it has been assumed that 30 per cent, 40 per cent or 50 per cent of the parent's joint Assessable Incomes should be allocated to child maintenance. Those percentages of joint income are substantially higher than the courts would historically have considered appropriate for child maintenance alone. So they have clearly been pitched at levels which include significant support for the Parent with Care. But the higher the income of the Parent with Care, and the lower the income of the Absent Parent, the more bizarre become the overall end results.

At the outset it was thought that the Agency's formulae would seldom result in Absent Parents having to pay out more than 30 per cent of assessable income. Real life has proved otherwise. So after April 1995 no Absent Parent will be required to pay more than 30 per cent of Assessable Income – or 33 per cent if payments include arrears, even if the arrears accumulated before the limit. This cap on payments further emphasises the point made above: requiring Absent Parents to pay 30 per cent of their income implies that Child Support is based on 60 per cent of the parents' joint incomes. And that base substantially exceeds any which the courts would historically have considered appropriate for child maintenance alone.

The courts might be able to remedy wildly anomalous results in cases where maintenance is still payable between the parents (ie the parents are or were married, there has been no clean break settlement, and the parent with the lower income has not remarried) – see also Chapter 6, page 92. But because of the basic approach which underlies Child Support neither they nor anyone else can do anything about other cases.

The basic elements of Child Support calculation can be summarised as in Table 1 on page 50.

Now we turn to the essential components – Assessable Income and the Maintenance Requirement.

Assessable Income

From the information supplied the Agency calculates the weekly Assessable Income of both parents.

These are the stages involved in that calculation:

1. Determine the parent's weekly net income:
    (a) Add up the parent's total gross weekly income from all sources.
    (b) Deduct from that total the amount which that parent has to pay weekly by way of income tax and National Insurance contributions plus half of any superannuation or pension contributions payable.
    (c) The parent's weekly net income is what remains.
2. Determine the parent's weekly exempt income:
    Exempt income is the amount which the regulations say a parent must retain to cover his or her own basic living expenses. Deductions, most of which are tied to current DSS Income Support allowances, are conditional on the circumstances of the parent being such that that parent would qualify for those allowances if he or she claimed Income Support.

Table 1: *Child Support calculation*

Income calculation

1. Calculate total gross income from all sources

Deduct

Tax, National Insurance and half pension payments

Result

2. Total net income

Deduct

Exempt income

Result

3. Assessable Income

Child Support calculation

1. Calculate the maintenance requirement.
2. Child Support is half of Assessable Income up to the point where that half equals the Maintenance Requirement; *plus* 15 per cent, 20 per cent or 25 per cent (depending on the number of children) of any balance of Assessable Income above that so required – but limited to 30 per cent of the Absent Parent's Assessable Income after April 1995.

Exempt income is the total of the following:
(a) The DSS Income Support Adult Personal Allowance – £45.70 a week in 1994/95 – plus,
(b) The DSS Income Support Disability Premium and Severe Disability Premium if they would be claimable, plus,
(c) If the parent concerned has a child living with him or her, where that parent is father or mother, the DSS Family Premium, plus the DSS Income Support personal allowance appropriate to a child of that age, plus the appropriate DSS Disabled Child Premium for a disabled child. But:

- These deductions are halved if the parent lives with a new partner, the child is the fruit of the new partnership, and the new partner has a net income greater than the total of that partner's Income Support allowances.
- There is no allowance for children of whom the parent is not father or mother, eg step-children.

  Plus,

(d) If the parent concerned has a child which qualifies under (c) above but no new partner living with him or her, the DSS Income Support Lone Parent and Carer Premiums, plus,

(e) The amount of the parent's reasonable weekly costs for housing the parent and any of that parent's own children living with him or her, eg rent, mortgage repayments, payments for residential care etc. But:

- Subject to some exceptions housing costs of an Absent Parent are regarded as unreasonable if they exceed £80 a week or half that parent's net income (whichever is greater).
- Even if reasonable, before April 1995 Absent Parents were only allowed the full amount of their housing cost if they lived alone or alone with children of which they were father or mother. In all other cases Absent Parents were only allowed to deduct fixed percentages of their housing cost – the percentage being determined by who else shared the accommodation. Thus, a remarried Absent Parent was allowed 75 per cent of housing costs if there were no children; 82.14 per cent if there were two children of which that parent was father or mother; but only 53.57 per cent if there were two step-children. After April 1995 housing costs will not be discounted for new families – but subject to further discretionary adjustment after 1996/97 (see 'Discretionary appeals', pages 54–5).

  Plus,

(e) After April 1995 *employed* (but not self-employed) parents will be allowed excessive costs of travel to work – at 10p per mile for every mile by which the straight line distance between home and work exceeds 150 miles a week. After 1996/97 either parent may seek further discretionary adjustment of any such allowance and further allowance for excess travel needed to maintain contact with children (see 'Discretionary appeals', pages 54–5).

3. Determine the parent's assessable income:

   Subtract exempt income from net income. Assessable Income is what is left.

The Maintenance Requirement

The Maintenance Requirement is the basic target figure for Child Support. It is the sum of the following DSS Income Support allowances (usually reviewed annually) less basic Child Benefit (formerly Family Allowance):

1. The age-related child allowance for each child.
2. The Family Premium.
3. As long as at least one child is under 16, a proportion at least of the adult Personal Allowance – 100 per cent until the youngest child is 11; 75 per cent until the youngest is 14; and 50 per cent until the youngest reaches 16.
4. Lone Parent Premium – unless the Parent with Care is living with a new partner.

Using April 1994 rates the Agency's publication 'A Guide to Child Support Maintenance' gives the following example for two children aged 9 and 12 living in a single parent family:

1.	DSS Child Allowances	£38.65
2.	Family Premium	10.05
3.	Lone Parent Premium	5.10
4.	Adult Allowance	45.70
	Total	99.50
5.	Less basic Child Benefit (£10.20 for first child; £8.25 for second – additional one-parent benefit is not deducted)	18.45
	Maintenance Requirement	81.05

Note that part of items 2. and 3. and all of item 4. involve maintenance for the Parent with Care and not the children; also that where Assessable Income exceeds that required to cover the Maintenance Requirement, the percentages of Assessable Income then added to Child Support (15, 20 or 25 per cent – see pages 47–8) exceed the proportions of income which the courts would historically have been likely to allow for child maintenance alone, and so also include an element of adult maintenance.

Poverty trap avoidance

(a) Absent Parents

It was realised from the outset that as calculated, Child Support might reduce Absent Parents and their new families to below basic DSS subsistence levels.

The regulations therefore also include a long stop – again based on DSS Income Support allowances. An Absent Parent is entitled to retain as his or her protected income a weekly sum sufficient to equal the total of:

1. £30 plus the amount of Income Support allowances which would be payable for the Absent Parent and all those dependent on that parent in his or her household – including any step-children.
2. If the whole family's income exceeds the total in 1. above, 15 per cent of the excess.
3. Any part of the household's reasonable housing costs which does not arise from mortgage repayments.
4. The household's Council Tax liability.

A Child Support assessment must be limited to such amount as leaves an Absent Parent's protected income intact.

(b) Parents with Care

Originally, Child Support offered nothing to Parents with Care still relying on DSS means-tested benefits – the DSS took the lot. After April 1997 such parents will be 'credited' with the amount of Child Support actually paid but only up to a maximum of £5 a week and will be able to claim the accumulated saving if they start working for more than 16 hours a week.

Child Support and high incomes

The amount of Child Support which can be assessed on top of that required to cover the Maintenance Requirement (ie at the rate of 15 per cent, 20 per cent or 25 per cent of Assessable Income dependent on the number of children) is subject to an upper limit.

That limit was arrived at by adding together the current Income Support Family Premium and the (age dependent) personal allowance which would be made for the child on Income Support and multiplying the total by 3.

At 1994 rates the allowance for a child aged between 11 and 15 was £23.00 and Family Premium was £10.05. So the maximum weekly Child Support which could be assessed on top of the Maintenance Requirement for a single child in that year was £99.15 – £5,155.80 a year. To reach that maximum (at 15 per cent deduction rate) an Absent Parent would have to have an Assessable Income on top of that taken to cover the Maintenance Requirement which exceeded £34,476 per annum – and significantly more with two or more children.

After April 1995 the maximum will be halved but there will still not be many cases where Child Support is limited – and of course, the right to go to the courts for more anyway remains.

Special cases

1. *Children in care of neither parent.* Child Support may be assessed against both parents if their child is in the care of a third party. The assessment against each is made in exactly the same way, but Lone Parent Premium is excluded from the Maintenance Requirement if the child is in institutional care.
2. *Children dividing their time between both parents.* Child Support may also be adjusted proportionally if a child spends at least 104 nights a year (two nights a week) in the household of the 'absent' parent, but there is no adjustment for lesser periods.
3. *Children of the same parent in the care of different people and of different parents in the care of the same person.* Child Support may also be adjusted if the children of an Absent Parent are in the care of different people, or if a Parent with Care is looking after the children of different Absent Parents. Such cases are rare. Their particular detailed implications are best established by direct contact with the Agency, and so are not further explored here.

Discretionary appeals

Basic Child Support rules are rigid and inflexible. After 1996/97 officers of the Agency (and on appeal the Child Support Appeal Tribunal) will have a limited discretion to allow for exceptional problems in defined cases.

Absent Parents will be able to seek relief if they face hardship because the formulae do not adequately take account of:

- Travel costs to work or to maintain contact with a child.
- Expenses resulting from illness or disability.
- Exceptional costs of caring for a step-child.
- Debts incurred before separation.
- The value of property transferred before April 1993.
- Obligations which were taken on because it was assumed that a maintenance agreement made before April 1993 would govern the future circumstances of the parents.
- Any of the matters for which a Parent with Care can seek adjustment under (ii)–(iv) below.

Parents with Care will be able to seek similar relief if:

- They are not allowed sufficient deductions in respect of any of the matters allowed to Absent Parents as listed above.
- The Absent Parent has assets or an extravagant life style which belie assessed income.
- The Absent Parent can in fact afford housing costs, or has deliberately inflated them, or has a new partner who could or should be able to meet or help with them.
- The Absent Parent is able to meet travel costs or has deliberately inflated them.
- Any allowance for property transferred is too generous.

Enforcement

If an Absent Parent fails to pay Child Support, the Agency can order his employer to deduct what is due from his wages and pay it direct.[3] If he is not employed, or a deduction order is not effective, the Agency can apply to the courts for a Liability Order for what is due. On any such application the courts must accept the Agency's assessments of Child Support due.[4]

Liability Orders can then be enforced by any of the procedures available for recovering court judgment debts.[5] (See also Chapter 8, pages 129–30).

Until payment Absent Parents are liable to pay interest on any arrears which have accumulated. After 1996/97 a system of penalties for late payment is to be substituted.

Notes

1. Section 8(6), 8(7) and 8(8) Child Support Act
2. Section 6(2) Child Support Act
3. Sections 31, 32 Child Support Act
4. Section 33(4) Child Support Act
5. Sections 35–40 Child Support Act

Chapter 4

The General Law on Property and Maintenance

Chapter 3 dealt with the separate special jurisdiction of the Child Support Agency which now dominates questions of child maintenance.

Now we turn to the powers which the courts retain to order:

1. Maintenance between adults.
2. Maintenance for 'children of the family' – children whom a married person has accepted as members of his or her family of whom that parent is not the natural or adoptive parent, ie step-children. Any natural parent of such children will anyway be liable to assessment of Child Support for such children – as described in Chapter 3. And the courts must take any such support into account before determining any additional step-parent liability. But if step-parents' marriages founder they may still have to maintain any children of their family if their means substantially exceed those of natural parents, or if natural parents cannot be traced, or have died.
3. Additional maintenance for natural or legally adopted children on top of Child Support – but only after Child Support has first been assessed. Such maintenance is only likely if the relevant parent has very substantial means (see Chapter 3).
4. Lump sum, property transfer and other property settlements between spouses, which may only be ordered after decree nisi in divorce – or nullity – cases.
5. Lump sum, property transfer and other property settlements in favour of children. Such orders may only be made as part of the maintenance arrangements for a child until he or she reaches the age of 18 – lifelong provision is not what they are about. And they are rare if the parents are or were married; in such cases property settlements are usually confined to the parents. But where the parents were not married the courts have no power to order either parent to settle property on the other, and in such cases they are increasingly likely to order settlements in favour of children which

57

serve their interest.[1]

6. Property adjustments between unmarried cohabitees. The law governing the rights of spouses (people who are or were married) and children differs radically from that which applies to and between unmarried couples. So we shall look first at the position of spouses and children. The legal position of cohabitees is then summarised on page 68.

Spouses and children

Sections 22, 23, 24 and 24A of the Matrimonial Causes Act 1973 (summarised above) define the types of order which courts can make. Sections 25 and 25A (summarised below but the precise words appear in Appendix 1) indicate how they must set about it. But these sections only contain broad guiding principles. The techniques used to translate principles into mathematically precise results are left to customary practice – of which more below.

Section 25 of the 1973 Act contains the guidelines for calculating the *amount* of financial provision. Section 25A contains the guidelines for deciding the *duration* of maintenance – how long it should be paid.

Deciding the amount of financial provision

The law on the calculation of the amount of maintenance or capital provision is essentially this:

1. The court must have regard to all the circumstances of the case, first consideration being given to the welfare while a minor of any child of the family who has not attained the age of 18.
2. The court must in particular have regard to:
   (a) the income, earning capacity, property and other financial resources which the parties have or are likely to have in the foreseeable future; this includes any increase in earning capacity which the court considers either party might reasonably acquire
   (b) the parties' financial needs, obligations and responsibilities, existing or foreseeable
   (c) the family's standard of living before the marriage broke down
   (d) the age of the parties and the duration of the marriage
   (e) any disability of either party
   (f) the contributions which the parties have made or are likely to

make to the family's welfare, including contributions by way of looking after the home and family

(g) the parties' conduct – if the court thinks it would be inequitable to disregard it

(h) if the marriage is to be dissolved (in divorce and nullity cases) the value of pension benefits which either party will lose when they cease to be a spouse.

There are two additional lists which come into play when financial provision for children is under consideration – one for the spouses' own children and an additional one for children of the family. In the case of the spouses' own children they add to (a), (b), (c) and (e) above the following:

- the financial needs of the child
- the child's income, earning capacity, property and financial resources
- any disability of the child
- the way the child was being educated and trained and the way its parents expected it to be.

In the case of children of the family there is then a further list for consideration:

- whether the spouse against whom maintenance is sought actually assumed any responsibility for the children's maintenance – and if he (or she) did, on what basis and for what period
- if a responsibility was assumed, whether the person who assumed it knew that the child was not his
- whether anyone else is liable to maintain the child – eg by Child Support.

This is the essence of what the law says about the calculation of maintenance and the determination of who shall have what property – the calculation of amounts. It does not lay down any percentages. It does not indicate that any of the principles have any particular priority over the others.

Before 1970 the law contained no guidelines of substance. Courts were required to do what they considered just and reasonable and things of that nature. Most of the components of Section 25 came from previous decisions in individual cases. There was, for example, a long line of cases to the effect that maintenance should not exceed that necessary to enable a wife receiving it to maintain her previous standard of living. Those cases gave rise to the part of Section 25 which requires a court to 'have regard' to the parties' previous standard of living. But inevitably previous standard of living only has any real relevance to cases where the parties are so rich that it is possible to consider sustaining it despite the division of resources.

Many of the other parts of Section 25 came from cases involving similarly limited circumstances, but Section 25 now says that all the principles shall be considered in all cases. Indeed, judges frequently emphasise the fact on appeal, though often only when deciding to give a particular principle greater weight than it seems to have been given in the decision under appeal.

Thus, on the face of it, the law still effectively gives individuals, magistrates, magistrates clerks, solicitors, barristers, Registrars and judges *carte blanche* to reach decisions which embody little more than their personal gut reaction to the family's circumstances, however much that reaction may be informed by practice and experience. For there is hardly ever a case where it is not possible to latch on to some particular aspect of a family's affairs which matches a phrase or phrases sets out in the long list of things for which 'first consideration' or 'regard' is required.

The published law reports contain many examples of cases where courts have decided that a particular principle justifies more or less. In virtually all of them the judges go on to add, however, that each case must be taken on its own and that their decision should not be taken as a precedent for any other case. The official result is that, unlike every other field of English law, decisions in family law do not bind or guide anyone in considering any future similar case. It is therefore necessary to consider the realities.

The published law reports only cover the small number of cases which reach the higher courts and are always concerned with appeals from lower courts – typically from the decisions of magistrates, a County Court Registrar or judge. Moreover, the small proportion of cases which reaches the higher courts allows judges plenty of time to indulge elegant intellectual exercises involving the balancing of differing values of all the phrases in Section 25 and the semantics of those phrases. And although they periodically express anxiety about the cost of it all, they do not have to pay it – as you may have to if your case ends up before them.

So while judges may speak with affection of an exercise which allows them, as they would see it, to fine tune the 'justice' of particular decision to particular cases – even if none of them would fine tune the same case in the same way – such fine tuning is not likely to be an art which will be deployed unless your case ends up before a High Court judge. Lacking any other guidance, lesser legal luminaries will still use guidelines in decided cases, precedent or not.

Because of the cost, and often also because spouses are emotionally drained after one appearance in court, the vast majority of decisions on financial matters in family law cases are reached by negotiated agreement or made by the courts below High Court level. And the solicitors, barristers, magistrates (in the case of Family Proceedings Court cases) and County Court Registrars do not have time for the High Court judge's approach. A solicitor or barrister specialising in family law, and the family bench of a busy magistrates court, may have to advise on, or decide, hundreds of financial cases every year. A County Court Registrar may have to decide thousands. These lawyers have no time to play around with the abstruse, and often conflicting, values in Section 25. They may, in a particularly glaring case, try to give some extra weight to a particular principle. But if they do, they may not say that they have done so; and if they do say, they are not likely to identify precisely what difference it has made to the numbers they would otherwise have thought of.

In the large majority of cases they will not look beyond the hard figures – incomes and asset values. They will then apply to those hard figures whatever formulae and principles they have themselves developed and favoured idiosyncratically over the years, and their decision will be the result. Quite simply, there is no other way in which people dealing with a large volume of cases and decisions can hope to do it in a manner which seems consistent to them.

So the formulae and principles used are not defined by law. They are likely to vary in detail, and sometimes in substance, individual by individual. In most cases their similarity will probably be sufficient to lead to a result which is more or less in the same parish as any similar lawyer would reach. But that may still be a very large parish leaving plenty of room for further costly debate as to how one eliminates the gaps between its villages.

For these reasons much space is devoted in the chapters which follow to points which may help you to get into that parish and then reach firm conclusions without that cost. Wherever possible, leading lights are set from established practice and court decisions, and references are given to cases so that you may look at them yourself. Where a range of circumstances lies between the points where leading lights exist, suggestions are made as to how you may establish specific answers within that range. For example, practice may involve fairly specific ideas as to maintenance where one spouse has no income and where the spouses have equal incomes, but with very little in between.

The idea that decisions on maintenance and other financial provision may be dominated by what there is and by the application of preconceived notions as to how you should share it, often to the exclusion of other factors, may horrify you but, frankly, it reflects no more than another recognition of reality. For the reality is that the income and other resources which you and your partner have define the outer limits of what can be done. Whatever orders are made or not made, a court can, at the end of the day, at best change the percentages in which you share it; and unless you have so much that it is possible to carve it up and leave the ways of life of both untouched, both of you are bound to end up worse off and calculations which roughly equate the hardship may be all anyone can achieve.

But should the hardship be equated?

This brings us to the one factor which weighs on the minds of spouses when they part more than any other: why should I pay so much, or receive so little when my partner has behaved so badly? After all, one of the matters which Section 25 actually requires the court to have regard to is 'the conduct of each of the parties, if that conduct is such that it would in the opinion of the court be inequitable to disregard it'.

So let us look specifically at conduct.

The effect of conduct on financial provision

You may well feel that your spouse's behaviour has been outrageous. He or she may feel the same about you. But the first problem which others face is that behaviour in any relationship is part of a series of events, the first giving rise to the next and so on. No one can even begin to think objectively about them without looking at the whole series. The next problem is that of weighing the respective behaviour of both parties. It may be quite clear that both have contributed: but where is the scale pan in which one can balance the separate contributions of each and decide not only if one is heavier than the other, but how much heavier it is?

In the earlier history of divorce everything was simpler, but only because specific acts were labelled as bad; and because divorce and associated law originally evolved in a criminal law atmosphere – indeed, actions based on adultery were originally called actions for Criminal Conversation. So it followed logically (if not rationally) that a person guilty of bad conduct should be punished by having to pay more. But family law is not now dealt with as a matter of crime, nor is it dealt with on the same simplistic bases that concepts of crime and punishment invite. And the modern reality is that rarely, if ever, will the conduct of the parties, as such, during and up to the breakdown of marriage be regarded as capable of any measurement which makes any difference to financial provision.

If a marriage has collapsed a very short time after it was celebrated, no financial provision may be awarded;[2] but this is more because neither partner has materially changed his or her premarital financial position than because the conduct of either of them has resulted in a swift end to the relationship. If a marriage has continued for some time, no one is likely to be able to put any differential weight on the conduct of the parties. Unless that can be done, conduct is irrelevant.

Magistrates have sometimes taken a simpler view of conduct, perhaps because they also deal with criminal cases where they often have to. They did in a case in 1982 where a wife had left her soldier husband four years after they married, while he was overseas, and considered that as conduct sufficient to deny her claim to maintenance.[3] But the special training which Family Proceedings Court magistrates receive is now likely to iron out such differences of attitude. Generally, conduct is only likely to enter into the question at all where it has caused some actual financial disability (violence which has maimed a spouse, for example) or where it is extreme by any standard. That was held to be so in a case where a wife, hoping to gain financially, did nothing to prevent her husband's attempt at suicide after he had discovered her adulterous affair; and in another case where a wife was sent to prison for attempting to murder her husband. But even in such cases, though losing any right to maintenance, spouses may still qualify for a share in their joint property.[4]

The general message therefore has to be that you are unlikely to gain anything but an increased bill for costs if you fight for conduct-related prizes in the financial stakes at the end of a marriage.

The duration of maintenance orders

The basic obligation to pay maintenance to a spouse continues until that spouse dies or remarries. The basic obligation to maintain a child continues until the child reaches the age of 17 but may be extended so long as the child remains in full-time education.

But a spouse's right to maintenance may end with a clean break order. Clean breaks are dealt with in detail in Chapter 8. But we will look here at the law which defines the court's power to put time-limits to maintenance, and maintenance-related obligations (eg maintenance secured on property – *secured maintenance*).

Time-limits on maintenance for spouses

The declared object of the law is to encourage a clean break between spouses, but as with so many matters in divorce that is often not how it seems to work out in practice.

Essentially what Section 25A (added to the 1973 Act in 1984) says is:

1. When considering financial provision after decree nisi of divorce or decree of nullity the courts must consider whether to exercise their powers (and this usually means the powers relating to ongoing provision such as maintenance) in such a way as to terminate financial obligations between the parties.
2. If a court considers that there is no case for ongoing provision, it can dismiss any application for it and order that no further application can be made.
3. If it considers that there is a case for ongoing provision, it may nevertheless limit that provision to such period as it considers sufficient to allow the recipient of that to adjust to the ending of financial dependence without undue hardship – ie impose an end date to maintenance.

Section 25A has encouraged many couples to agree clean breaks which the courts have then approved. But the courts have proved far less willing to order clean breaks in the hard core cases which go to court in the absence of agreement. For example, in 1988[5] the Court of Appeal considered the case of Mr Lewis Whiting. He was then 53, he had become redundant in 1983 and had had a low income since. His 48-year-old wife was employed full time as a teacher on a salary exceeding £10,000 a year. An original maintenance order in her favour had been reduced to a nominal 5p a year when be became redundant. Four years later he applied for it to be extinguished on the clean break basis.

The local County Court Registrar refused his application. So did the Court of Appeal when he appealed. Lord Justice Slade said:

> 'With Mrs Whiting earning more than Mr Whiting, there were strong arguments in favour of the 5p order being discharged. However, it could not be assumed that her independence would continue indefinitely. Judges were entitled to take the view that a maintenance order should be kept alive in case unforeseen contingencies deprived a wife of the ability to provide for herself.'

Now it must be quite clear that if the courts are generally going to allow for the unforeseeable, and to give it greater weight than facts which are patent at the time, Section 25A is a dead letter. There can never be any case whose future may not be affected by something unforeseeable.

So, since we must assume that it is not the intention of the courts to ignore the law altogether, when may end dates to maintenance reasonably be expected if the parties do not agree?

It helps perhaps first to identify two cases when they may not:

1. If a marriage has run for many years, one spouse is well established and the other spouse has not had any significant employment, the chances of the latter becoming self-supporting must be small. In that case one would not expect any time-limit on maintenance.
2. If there are children still at school, under school age or disabled of any age, the prospects of the spouse with their care becoming self-supporting are inevitably restricted until the children are no longer dependent, unless that spouse already has an occupation which clearly allows self-sufficiency. That may be the case with some professional occupations but it is not likely to be the case with any other. Only when the children cease to be dependent may it be appropriate to consider time-limits.

End dates – immediate or after a defined period – may, however, still be relevant in the following cases:

1. Where the marriage – or the time during which the spouses have lived together – has been of short duration and marriage has not made any significant difference to the capacity of the spouses to support themselves as they did before marriage. Although the principle has certainly not been followed universally the courts have ruled that there is no case for financial provision after marriages of short real duration.[6] And the duration of the marriage is one of the multitude of areas to which the court is required to have regard anyway under Section 25. Yet even with short marriages there is a problem with late marriages and remarriages between people of advancing years where one partner is well established and the other is not and is never likely to be. It may be that the marriage has not made a blind bit of difference to the financial prospects of the latter; and logically they should not acquire a charter for their support for the rest of their days simply through the accident of marriage. But that logic may not appeal to a court if the marriage fails. So those contemplating first, second or subsequent marriages in later life should beware the hazards of unestablished spouses, particularly because the failure rate of

such marriages is high.

2. Where the spouses are already established in employment or businesses which already yield them broadly comparable incomes. One would not expect maintenance of any substance in such a case, and, despite the Court of Appeal's decision in *Whiting* v *Whiting*, it seems unreasonable that options should be kept open merely to guard against the unforeseeable.

3. Where the parties have sufficient capital or property to allow additional capital provision to compensate for the absence of maintenance.

On the duration of maintenance Scottish law contrasts starkly with English (see Appendix 2: Section 9(1)(d) and (e) Family Law (Scotland) Act 1985).

In Scotland the basic rule is that an award of maintenance shall be such as is reasonable to enable the recipient to adjust to the loss of support following divorce over a period of not more than three years after the dissolution of the marriage.

Only if the divorce is likely to cause serious financial hardship can the provision be for an undefined 'reasonable period'.

But obviously both these provisions envisage that a specific period will still be defined.

English law is not precise and offers no such guidance to individuals or their advisers. But if individuals choose to follow the general guidelines outlined above – even the more specific ones existing under Scottish law – their result is not likely to be so far distant from what lawyers might negotiate or courts order that they will profit by risking the costs of fighting about it.

Time-limits on maintenance for children

The duration of maintenance for children is precise and the position of children of the unmarried is the same as that of the married.

The basic rule is simple:

1. Any child maintenance order is made in the first instance to run until the child attains the age of 17.

2. If a child continues in full-time education after the age of 17, the court may order that maintenance continues until the child ceases in full-time education. Applications for extended maintenance are usually made by the parent with the care of the children but in certain circumstances children over 18 may themselves apply.[7]

3. Child Support assessed by the Child Support Agency runs for comparable periods (see Chapter 3).

No reported decisions of the courts spell out the criteria on which child maintenance orders in the courts may be extended beyond 17 and a great deal may depend on the individual prejudices of the legal functionary who considers them. For example, a Registrar who takes the view that a parent should not be required to pay when grants are available, may decide that enough is enough. On the other hand, one who feels that the burden on the public purse should be reduced by parental contribution may order maintenance.

Equally, idiosyncratic judgments may be applied to the worthiness of the proposed further education, particularly if the parent with care of the child seems to have encouraged objectives which are exotic and seem unlikely to be productive of any great future advantage.

So, for example, when considering an application to support a girl in a further education drama course, a Registrar once observed: 'Well I don't think much of that. I don't see that that's going to do the girl much good. She'd be better off getting a job. I'm not going to order her father to pay for it.'

One always hopes that by the time the question of further education arises both parents have consulted over a period of time and both have developed a sufficiently good relationship to reach common and reasonable agreed conclusions about what should be done.

But that does not always happen. And it is unfortunate that applications to extend maintenance beyond the age of 17 are most common in cases where spouses are still bitterly locked in the battles of their former marriage; and spouses who make applications all too often regard them as another way to keep the battle alive. With public grants for further education now radically curtailed, obtaining further maintenance may be the only option. And Child Support via the Child Support Agency will be automatic if its rules so provide. But otherwise a spouse with the care of children does not *have* to ask for more.

The sequence of financial decisions in the courts

It may not be possible to establish the incomes of the parties until the destination of property has been decided; property may create income or deductions from income (eg mortgage interest) which have to be included in the computations of the parties' incomes before maintenance can be calculated. Equally, the maintenance which may be payable may mandate what happens to property: a house may have to be sold and its proceeds divided if the divided incomes of the parties, including any maintenance, will not allow either of them to continue paying a mortgage. The following three chapters deal separately with the law and practice on income, property, maintenance and property reallocation but you will have to remember that it may not always be possible to do that in practice. You may have to decide how property is to be shared before you can calculate maintenance; you may then have to go back to the property shares you first thought of if the maintenance makes the property position difficult.

The unmarried

The unmarried have no legal right to claim maintenance against each other, though they may be able to claim provision for their maintenance out of the estate of an unmarried partner who died while they were still living together (see also Chapter 9). They may have the right to claim property or a share in property, but that right derives from the general law of trusts, and in particular from the extent to which the unmarried have contributed in cash or something which has the value of cash (helping to build a house, for example) to the property. These rights are considered more fully in Chapters 5 and 7.

Notes

1. See *K* v *K* (1992) *The Times* 21 February; in Re *F* (minors) (parental home ouster) (1993) *The Times* 1 December
2. *Krystman* v *Krystman* (1973) *The Times* 29 March
3. *Robinson* v *Robinson* (1982) *The Times* 30 October
4. *Kyte* v *Kyte* (1987) *The Times* 17 August; *Evans* v *Evans* (1988) *The Times* 8 August
5. *Whiting* v *Whiting* (1988) *The Times* 29 January
6. *T* v *T* (1974) *The Times* 2 November
7. Section 15 and Para 2 First Schedule, Children Act 1989

Chapter 5

What Income and Property? The Starting Point for Financial Calculations under the General Law

Maintenance transfers income from the spouse or parent who has more to the spouse or child who has less. Property transfer and lump sum orders are used to alter imbalances in their capital. Remember that women as well as men may have to pay in appropriate circumstances. Chapter 4 dealt with the principles which the law lays down to govern these exercises. Chapters 6 and 7 describe how it is actually done. The process involves looking at the existing incomes and capital of the people involved, establishing the gaps which lie between them, and using court orders to change, diminish or extinguish those gaps.

So before you can get anywhere you have to define exactly what income and capital each of you have. That is what this chapter is about.

You may think that it is relatively simple, assuming everyone is straightforward, to determine what the existing incomes and capital of you, your partner and your children are. But in practice that is often one of the most time-consuming and, if you employ solicitors, costly parts of the whole task in deciding financial provision.

If either of you is less than straightforward, there may be no way of avoiding that cost. If you try to hide income or assets, or to massage the figures, you may leave your partner no choice but to employ a solicitor to use the very extensive powers which the law provides to discover the truth. The chances are that, in the end, it will be discovered, but at very considerable cost, which you may have to pay. Moreover, if a court is satisfied that you have concealed facts, it may estimate what is involved. So you have little to gain from anything less than the truth – and a great deal to lose, however attractive the thought of getting away with something may seem.

But if you and your partner are able to agree and be satisfied about everything (and the rest of this chapter is designed to help you do that) you still need to bear in mind the points made about the duties of your solicitors, if you have them, under the General Warnings in Chapter 1. Unless you instruct them specifically to the contrary, they will still have to go through all the exercises necessary to verify your figures, and the cost of doing so may well be very similar to the cost of finding out in the first place.

Let us then turn to the problem of deciding how much there is. Income has to be established in all cases involving maintenance. Total assets have to be established in the case of claims between married couples or with cohabitees if they were living together when the first of them died, and the survivor claims on his or her estate (see also Chapter 9, pages 137–40).

What is income for the purposes of calculating maintenance under the general law?

Income actually received

All income actually received or receivable comes into account when maintenance is calculated. The main likely sources of income and some of the information which may help to establish it are set out in the checklist at the end of this section (see pages 75–7). Note that if you are entitled to have Child Support assessed by the Child Support Agency (see Chapter 3) the amount of that support must be added to your income and deducted from the income of the parent liable to pay it before arriving at the totals on which general maintenance is calculated.

Where children have income that also is taken into account.[1]

Since 1977 the courts have emphasised that maintenance calculations must be based on the real income of the people involved – ie that which is available after unavoidable expenses have been deducted from it – and not merely on their nominal gross income before tax. It is the net – or real – effect of orders which matters.[2]

Tax is not the only unavoidable liability to be deducted before arriving at the income figures on which maintenance is to be calculated. But here there is another difficulty. So far no court or Act of Parliament has spelled out definitively and exhaustively what other deductions should be made – though the 1991 Child Support Act does that for Child Support calculations (see Chapter 3, pages 49–51). Nevertheless some principles are clear.

Because tax is deductible, it is clearly logical that any payment allowed as a deduction in calculating tax should also be allowed in calculating maintenance. Pension, superannuation and qualifying life assurance payments are examples – though there may be room for argument about capital allowances claimed against taxable income by the self-employed if they absorb a sizeable slice of income. Other inescapable taxes and similar payments should also be deducted – National Insurance contributions are an example.

In addition, the courts have specifically extended the principle of deductions to include essential living costs such as mortgage interest.[3] And as mortgage interest is deductible so too is reasonable rent payable by those living in rented accommodation; and also any payment having the nature of a household tax – water rates, Council Tax and any further variations in local government taxation are examples.

In 1988, and because of the uncertainties, the Law Society's Family Law Committee was invited to express a view on the deductions which should be made from gross income before arriving at net income on which maintenance calculations should be based. The consensus of that committee, based on experience of court practice, was that deductions should embrace:

(a) The income tax payable by the parties.

(b) The National Insurance contributions which they are liable to pay.

(c) The travel costs which they have to pay to go to work.

(d) Pension or superannuation payments for which they are liable if there is to be ongoing maintenance (since the pension earned may in turn come into account for maintenance when it becomes payable); but not if the calculation is being made so that a clean break payment for forgoing maintenance can then be made (see Chapter 8) since there will not be any ongoing benefit in that case.

(e) Mortgage interest, rent and rates (or similar charge) payable but only insofar as these are reasonable and have not been inflated by an excessive commitment taken on in an attempt to reduce the maintenance liability.

To that list one must now add any Child Support assessable by the Child Support Agency. So if you are working out your own income and that of your partner and any children as a preliminary to calculating maintenance under the principles discussed in the next chapter you deduct those items from total gross income figures to arrive at the figures you work on.

Is actual income all that matters?

Actual income is not always the end of the story. In certain circumstances the incomes of payers or recipients available for calculation of maintenance may be treated as being larger or smaller because of extraneous factors. If you and your partner are concerned about some of these, their very nature may make it impossible for you to reach agreement, and you may have no choice but to face a full-scale maintenance battle involving solicitors. But on some of them at least you may be able to reach agreement. So apart from detailing the types of cases where notional adjustments, as we shall call them, may arise, we shall also look at such guidelines as are available.

Please note that it is only at this point that new wives, second wives or new cohabitees have any relevance. There is no separate or special code to cover second or subsequent marriages. The rights of a new family are only recognised to the extent that their essential needs diminish what can be paid to a previous family. And if your new family has resources of its own, it may be decided that you can afford to pay more to your previous family or need less from a previous partner. Equally, if a second or subsequent marriage breaks down, the rights of a spouse or children in that marriage are the same as those of a first spouse or children. They are only restricted to the extent that resources are already committed to former spouses or children.

Notional adjustments

Case 1: Where payer or recipient has a new partner

This is the most frequent, and often the most troublesome, case.
Essentially the position is this:

When you are liable to pay maintenance

(a) If you have new dependants (ie their own income is not enough to cover their own subsistence) the cost of sustaining your new family should be brought into account[4] and your income available for calculation of maintenance should be treated as less. There are no rules governing these calculations and one has to admit that some courts still seem to take the view that new families are a voluntary commitment and should not enter into account at all. However, the rates of support for individuals allowed by the DSS through Income Support are designed to cover bare subsistence. So it is logical at least that the appropriate rates of dependent adults or children (as the case may be) should be deducted from your income – less any net income which they actually have – before arriving at the base for calculating maintenance.

(b) If your new dependants have enough income to cover their own subsistence but no more, their existence is likely to be irrelevant. In the reverse case, for example, it has been decided that maintenance should not be reduced where a woman went to live with a man on low income.[5]

(c) If your new dependants have income greater than that needed to cover their own subsistence, it will be assumed that you do not have to spend as much on your own subsistence and can therefore spare more for maintenance.[6] But maintenance can still only come out of your income. New partners or children are not parties to the proceedings and no maintenance order can be made against them. In addition, they cannot themselves be compelled to disclose their resources although you may be required to. Of course, you cannot do this if your new family refuse to tell you what they are. But if that happens, a court may make what it regards as an educated guess, and educated guesses may prove more expensive than the truth.

So if you and your former partner are trying to cover this contingency, the simplest way is to try to agree some figure of 'extra' income to be added to your actual income in arriving at the base for maintenance calculation.

When you are entitled to maintenance

(a) If you remarry, you lose your right to maintenance by law.

(b) If you cohabit or have a new partner or children dependent on you, your former partner will not be ordered to pay more maintenance to help you support them, any more than his new family can, directly, be ordered to support you. But he may have to continue existing maintenance longer because your new commitments do not allow you to work.[7]

(c) If you cohabit and your new partner's resources suffice only to maintain him or her, it is not likely to make any difference to your maintenance (see Case 1(b) above).

(d) If you cohabit with someone with income which exceeds his or her subsistence needs, you may be presumed to be better off and the same adjustments should be made to your maintenance – or income – as apply in the reciprocal case. As an example, in a case involving capital, to which we still have to come, a wife's share in the former matrimonial home which was before the court but not resolved when she remarried, was limited to 8 per cent because she had married a rich man.[8]

Case 2: Where payer or recipient could earn more

It may be that there is an obvious prospect of greater income. More commonly, however, there has been a recent reduction in income – someone has stopped working overtime, has been ill and is only working part time, has been made redundant, or has given up working voluntarily. The essence in these cases is a change for the worse in income over a recent historical period which is why the record of incomes, particularly of the self-employed, may need to be looked at over a period of several years. If there is a genuine external cause for the change in income, usually supported by evidence from employers, doctors and so on it may make no difference – maintenance may be calculated on income as it is. But if it is reasonably clear that the fall in income has been consciously manipulated, maintenance may be calculated on income as it was – generally by taking an average over the period before the decline set in.

Case 3: Deliberate concealment

There are cases where the person claiming maintenance says that the payer's income figures do not tell the whole story.

Such allegations are most common with self-employed people and in some cases they are true: indeed, in happier years spouses may have discussed with each other tax and VAT frauds which all too often underlie this problem.

But they may arise in other cases – fiddling of expenses and concealment of tips are examples.

The problem with these cases is that they almost always involve a fraud on some third party. So allegations of concealment should not be raised without convincing evidence to support them. Nor should they be raised in any court proceedings unless the person raising them knows how the court will react. One Court Registrar said, for example, that if anyone proved such an allegation before him, it was his policy to send details to the investigation branch of the Inland Revenue immediately. And since that was likely to kill the goose which the person claiming maintenance hoped would lay a golden egg, that Registrar was not much troubled by people who said that income had not been fully disclosed. However, not all courts take that view and many confine themselves to judging the information before them. Caution and realism are essential but if there is more income, it should be declared.

Checklist for income

Here are listed various factors which may affect your own and your partner's incomes. If they exist, they should be included in the calculation of net income which forms the basis for maintenance calculations.

1. Add up the total of the following:
   (a) *Incomes from employment.* Certain perks – eg company cars – are assumed by the Inland Revenue to include a private benefit on which individuals pay tax. To the extent that they are, the value which is taxed should be treated as additional to income. Certificates from employers or the Inland Revenue usually provide sufficient back-up evidence.
   (b) *Profits from businesses.* Generally, accounts for the business for the three preceding years and tax assessments are the best indicators.
   (c) *Income from investments.* Building society and bank statements or books and share dividend warrants generally establish these. It is usually necessary to have details of all bank and other similar accounts and statements on them, not least to check back on payments which may disclose additional sources of income. It is important to remember that tax has already been deducted from many items of investment income – bank and building society deposit account interest and share dividends, for example – but that some payments, notably from National Savings accounts, may still be subject to tax.
   (d) *Family allowance.* Including the additional family allowance payable to children in single parent families and other social security benefits which are not means tested. Means tested benefits (Income Support and Family Support) will usually be reduced by the amount of any maintenance payable and should not enter into the recipient's account. But they are significant independent evidence of the means of payer or recipient, since they imply that his or her circumstances have been investigated in detail by the DSS. If anything has been concealed, criminal offences, prosecutable by the DSS, are also involved.

(e) *The amount of any Child Support receivable* (ie which the Child Support Agency could assess in your favour as described in Chapter 3).

(f) *The value in cash terms of any support available to you* from a new spouse, cohabitee or children accepted into your family – if they have resources which exceed their own basic subsistence needs.

2. Deduct from the total of the above the total of the following:

(a) *Income tax currently payable* and not already covered by the figures included in 1. above – it will be insofar as net after tax figures are used. The P60 tax form and payslips usually give the figures for the employed and the final tax assessment for the self-employed. For the latter a letter from the relevant Inspector of Taxes confirming the income and tax payable over, say, the last three years may be more straightforward.

Remember that tax payable may need to be adjusted to allow for changes in tax allowances which follow separation, eg the annual allowance (equal to the difference between the single person's and the married person's allowance) available to a person paying maintenance to a former spouse who has not remarried; the additional single parent allowance available to parents with care of children.

(b) *National Insurance payments*, including (for the self-employed) both the standard weekly amount and any additional profit-related Class IV National Insurance assessed and collected by the Inland Revenue.

(c) *Pension or superannuation payments*.

(d) *The reasonable cost of supporting a new spouse*, cohabitee or children living with and dependent on you.

(e) *Any child support* which you may have to pay under assessment by the Child Support Agency.

(f) *Mortgage interest* (or alternatively rent) payable for your accommodation. Many building society repayments include both capital and interest, so a letter from your building society may be needed to identify how much interest is paid. The limited tax relief on mortgage interest now available is usually deducted at source under MIRAS (Mortgage Interest Relief At Source) arrangements and the position of higher rate taxpayers is covered within their general tax assessment so net interest payable is what matters.

(g) *The amount of any rent, Council Tax and water rates payable on your accommodation*. Legally, rates have sometimes been held to be the responsibility of a husband even if a wife is occupying the property[9] but recently the person in occupation has been held liable.[10]

Cost of living calculations

What it costs to maintain your existing standard of living is only likely to have a significant bearing on the amount of maintenance if the incomes of you and your partner are such that you will both be able to maintain your living standards once you are separated but that cost is still generally useful for reference purposes.

Conclusion

All the items referred to above enter, or may enter, into the calculation of maintenance. Obviously, it is easier to end up with hard figures for items which have a precise origin – pay, tax, social security allowances and so on – than it is for notional ones such as the cost or value of new partners or children. But assuming a reasonable degree of honesty and goodwill, and even if it is only the peril of costs hanging over everyone which generates that honesty and goodwill, it ought to be possible for any two adults to arrive at mutually acceptable figures for their respective gross and net incomes, particularly if they have previously lived together and have even the minimal perception of the reality of each other's financial position which that usually involves.

Establishing gross and net incomes is the first, the most important, and sometimes (along with similar exercises on capital and property to which we now come) the most costly hurdle to be surmounted in the exercises leading to the calculation of maintenance to which we come in Chapter 6. So if you and your former partner can do that, you are well on your way to saving cost.

What are property and assets for the purposes of lump sum orders and property transfers?

As we saw in the last chapter, marriage gives its partners greater rights to share in property than cohabitees possess if they split up. If cohabitees stay together until one of them dies, the survivor may have a claim on the estate of the first to die; and in that circumstance all the property both of the estate, the survivor and other claimants may come into account (see Chapter 9). Otherwise property in issue between cohabitees is more limited. We will therefore deal first with the position of married or formerly married couples (bearing in mind that the same principles apply to cohabitees still living together when the first dies), and then with the position of cohabitees who split up during their lifetimes.

The married or formerly married

In England and Wales (but not now in Scotland) a court can make a lump sum or property transfer order which takes account of any property which husband and wife have, or indeed have the prospect of having, in the forseeable future – inheritances, even compensation received for personal injuries, may come into the reckoning.[11] In addition, if either of them has disposed of property in an attempt to defeat the claims of the other, a court can reverse the transaction and recover the property. Indeed, the courts have gone so far as to rule that such property can be recovered even from someone who acquired it in good faith, paid proper value for it, and had no actual knowledge that the transaction was intended to bypass a claim, if the circumstances were such that such intention should have been presumed.[12]

That is not to say that a court will necessarily regard all property as divisible in the same proportion – we come to the question of division later on in Chapter 7. But the starting point is and has to be what there is.

So if you are claiming or subject to a claim which relates to property, savings or any other capital, you will need to have details of, and to bear in mind, the following list:

Checklist of property

1. What property do each of you own in your own name – houses, furniture and other contents, cars, businesses, land, stock, shares, pension policies and rights, life insurances, cash, cash at banks, building societies or in other accounts? Do you have the right to have Child Support assessed in your favour by the Child Support Agency? Will such assessment include a lump sum payable to you in respect of arrears (see Chapter 3, page 42)?

2. If either of you is self-employed, you will probably be paying tax 12 months (sometimes more) in arrears under Schedule D and any savings you have will include sums which in due course will be payable to the Inland Revenue and should be deducted from those savings. What is the value of that tax liability?

3. What property do you own in joint names with your spouse or anyone else?

4. Did either of you own any of the property before you married or acquire it after you separated? Did any of it come by way of gift or inheritance from your families? If so, what property comes in these categories?

5. What are the current values of all the property involved? Will Capital Gains Tax be payable if any of it is sold and, if so, what is its value net of Capital Gains Tax? Is any of the property also used in a business belonging to either of you? Will there be a tax or other charge if it is sold and, if so, how much? Current published stock market figures are usually the best indicator of the value of quoted investments, and pension funds or pension insurance companies may be able to quote the values of pension rights. However, specific (and usually expensive) valuations may be required for other property, other than cash savings, unless these can be agreed between you and your partner. But bear in mind that a court is unlikely to order anything (sale, transfer, carve up or borrowing) which hazards a business that is the main source of family income and of any maintenance which can be paid. There is little point in going to war over such businesses; and any spouse who insists on costly valuations and accountant's investigations may end up with criticism from the court and the bill for the costs of the exercise.[13]

6. What mortgages exist in your name, your partner's or jointly, and how much is outstanding on them? Have payments due on mortgages or agreements been maintained, and, if not, what arrears are outstanding? What about balances outstanding on hire, hire purchase and credit sale agreements, joint or separate? Building societies or other lenders can usually supply these details.

7. What debts do you or your partner have, separate or joint? Will you have to pay a lump sum in respect of arrears of Child Support assessed by the Child Support Agency (see Chapter 3, page 42)? Are current accounts for public utility services – electricity, gas, telephone – in the name of the person who is using the service and who will continue to receive the bills and be liable for them unless or until the supplier is informed otherwise? If they are not, should you not make sure that they are?

8. If any transfer of property is involved, will the date or manner of

the transfer mean that a liability to Capital Gains Tax or Stamp Duty will arise? Can it be done in a way which avoids that liability? If not, what will it cost?

Essentially, you need to be able to establish exactly what each of you has, what it is worth, what your liabilities will be if it is sold (ie its net worth) and what your debts are. This will give you the picture of your total wealth, although, for the reasons we shall come to, not all property may be shared in the same way or be liable to be so shared.

Finally, while you are considering property you may also need to consider steps to preserve that property as it is until the situation can be sorted out. The following checklist will help you to do this.

Checklist of precautions to protect property until shares are divided

1. If you own property in joint names, is it held on terms which will result in your joint owner acquiring the lot automatically if you die – for example, a house in joint names held as 'joint tenants'; a joint banking account which either of you can sign? If it is, it may be wise for you to serve a notice (with a house) ending the joint tenancy immediately so that your share at least will pass to your estate if you die unexpectedly. Should you arrange for your bank to freeze any joint account?

2. Is there any property in the name of your spouse or former spouse alone? Have you done anything to prevent him or her disposing of it or mortgaging it without your approval before agreement can be reached or a court can consider the matter? If it is a house, for example, have you asked a solicitor to register a Class F Land Charge to warn off anyone who might buy or lend money on it? Have you served notices or applied for injunctions (as may be appropriate) to prevent other disposals? It may not be as important to take these steps if you are occupying the property or hold its title documents, but these may still not guarantee your protection if it is not in your name.

3. Until your marriage is actually dissolved by decree absolute your spouse will have the same rights under your will, or under the law of intestacy, as he or she would have had if you were still living happily together. Should you change your will, or make one, if you have not already done so?

These are issues which you and your spouse will have to consider if you have property of any sort, whether you try to settle your problems yourselves, or employ solicitors, or go to court about it. If you have property, beyond any doubt some of it will be hostage to costs and again they give you a powerful incentive to agree. But with that incentive you may be able to define and agree what there is, in whose name it is at present, and what it is worth – net of any costs and taxes which may arise on any realisation.

Cohabitees' property claims

As previously indicated, cohabitees have a narrower field for property claims and liabilities. Their rights are limited to that which they have acquired or provided themselves, that which is held in their own or joint names, and that to which they have made a financial contribution or a contribution in money's-worth. For example, a lady who helped her boyfriend with the work involved in building the bungalow which was to be their home was held to be entitled to a share in the value of the bungalow after they fell out.[14] Another lady and her daughter won shares in a house after they proved that they had contributed to the cost of mortgage repayments and improvements.[15]

Essentially, former cohabitees need to consider:

1. Property of any sort which they have acquired together.
2. Property which is jointly owned by them and their cohabitee.
3. The contributions they have made to property held by or in the name of their fellow cohabitee.
4. The values of any such property and of any outstanding mortgages or debts on it and of any taxes or costs which may arise if it is sold.

As with the married, action may be necessary to preserve cohabitees' property until shares in it can be decided. Cohabitees should also consider making wills and serving notices ending any joint tenancy of property (see the checklist of precautions on page 80). An application to the court for an injunction to prevent the disposal of property owned in the sole name of a fellow cohabitee may be the only way to guarantee that that property will not be disposed of prematurely.

Notes

1. *J* v *J* & *C* intervening (1989) *The Times* 7 February
2. *S* v *S* (1977) 1 All ER 56; also *Shallow* v *Shallow* (1978) 2 All ER 483;

    Furniss v *Furniss* (see 3 below); *Stockford* v *Stockford* (1982) 12 Fam
    Law 31

3. *Furniss* v *Furniss* (1981) *The Times* 29 October
4. See note 3 above
5. *Atkinson* v *Atkinson* (1987) *The Times* 12 August
6. *Brown* v *Brown* (1981) *The Times* 14 July; *Macey* v *Macey* (1981) *The Times* 14 July
7. *Fisher* v *Fisher* (1988) *The Times* 22 December
8. *H* v *H* (1974) *The Times* 19 June
9. *Regina* v *Harrow Justices* (1983) *The Times* 7 February
10. *Brown* v *Oxford* (1978) *The Times* 24 June; *Doncaster* v *Lockwood* (1987) *The Times* 15 January
11. *Michael* v *Michael* (1986) *The Times* 28 May; *Wagstaff* v *Wagstaff* (1991) *The Times* 26 November
12. *Kemmis* v *Kemmis* (1988) *The Times* 22 February
13. *P* v *P* (1989) *The Times* 3 February
14. *Cooke* v *Head* (1972) *The Times* 20 January
15. *Passee* v *Passee* (1987) *The Times* 8 August

Chapter 6

Calculating Maintenance under the General Law

Introduction

This chapter deals with the actual calculation of maintenance – between spouses and for children insofar as their position is not fully covered by Child Support – under the 1991 Child Support Act – see Chapter 3.

Obviously, the amount of maintenance has to be decided in any case where it has to be paid. But if a clean break deal or order is being considered between spouses, maintenance may also have to be calculated if the deal or order is to include an additional lump sum or property transfer to compensate for the absence of maintenance. Fuller details about possible compensatory calculations are given in Chapter 8.

The incomes of the payers and recipients of maintenance, and their children if the children have any income, are the starting point for maintenance calculations. When we talk about income or joint income we mean *net income* arrived at by the processes described in Chapter 5.

Maintenance is payable by and between 'Heads of Households' – people over 16 who are spouses (or former spouses) and/or are parents of children legally dependent on them.

If Heads of Households live alone the courts base maintenance decisions on their incomes and circumstances. If they live with a family the courts have regard to the incomes and circumstances of the whole family.

The basic objective of maintenance orders is to reduce differences between the incomes of Heads of Households who have more income and Heads of Households who have less – having regard also to the incomes and circumstances of any additional members of their families. But in pursuing that objective the courts have always recognised a simple reality – there is a limit to the total amount of maintenance which anyone can sensibly be ordered to pay. Exceed that limit and those liable to pay default on a massive scale. No legal system can cope with that – as experience with the now defunct Community Charge shows.

So levels of maintenance – for Heads of Households alone, or for them and their children – have always in practice been subject to such maximum limits as the courts considered reasonable. Those limits have never been specifically defined either in law or by the courts. But practice (referred to under 'The calculation of maintenance' below) illustrates where they lie.

The evolution of this approach had additional consequences. Because the courts' starting point was the total which could reasonably be ordered, it did not make much practical difference how that total was then carved up into specific orders in favour of spouses and dependent children where both were to be maintained. And because the courts' first task in history was to fix maintenance for dependent wives the usual approach, once children also came into the picture, was to apply the lions share of the available total to spousal maintenance, and what was left to children's orders. Thus children's orders, taken in isolation, often appeared lower than parental circumstances might suggest to be appropriate.

But such orders then tended to set an excessively low scale for children when the courts had to fix maintenance for them alone – as they did if parents were not married; as they have had to since 1969 if parents with care have remarried; and, since 1984, if parents have compromised their own positions with a clean break settlement (see also Chapter 8).

The 1991 Child Support Act has eliminated that hazard – indeed it has probably gone over the top in doing so (see Chapter 3). But since Child Support is now calculable and payable before the courts can do anything else, and before they can consider any other provision for children, the traditional approach is probably now appropriate to those questions of child maintenance which still rest with the courts.

The suggestions for calculating child maintenance set out under 'The calculation of maintenance' below are based on that view.

Conclusions from the history of maintenance

The law reports contain a very long record of court decisions on maintenance. It stretches back even before 1857, when divorce first became possible by application to a court rather than by private Act of Parliament, because maintenance almost always figured in High

Court decrees of judicial separation. All the early cases involved rich people – no one else could afford High Court proceedings. But, particularly after legal aid was introduced in 1949, average and poor families have figured increasingly in the record. Taking all the decisions together, it is clear that the courts adopt a basic general approach for average families; but if a family is very poor or very rich (so that straightforward mathematical calculations produce bizarre results) they then limit the maintenance which is ordered so as to avoid an excessive burden on the poor, or excessive generosity to the rich.

Who then is rich, poor or average? As usual there are no official rules but the following guidelines match the criteria which may be divined from decided cases and such practice of Registrars as is known:

1. Rich families are those whose total income is sufficient, whether or not it needs to be adjusted by maintenance, to make it possible for both halves of the divided family to continue to enjoy the standard of living which they enjoyed (or, in the case of previously stingy spouses, could have enjoyed) while they lived together.
2. Poor families are roughly those whose total *gross* income is at or below the average non-manual national wage – £18,174 gross in 1994. People may not think of themselves as poor if they are living together on that wage, but they certainly will be if they split up.
3. Average families lie between the two – they do not have enough income, whatever adjustments may be made by maintenance, to make sure that both halves of the divided family can continue to enjoy the same standard of living as they did together, but there is enough to avoid them being driven down towards subsistence level.

We start, therefore, with the principles used for the average family, since they provide the base line. After that we consider the cut-offs which may be applied to maintenance calculated on an average basis because the family is poor or rich.

The calculation of maintenance

The average family

Taking basic family circumstances – whether or not both spouses have income, in what proportions they have it, whether or not there are dependent children, if there are, who they are with, and whether maintenance is to be for children only or is also to include a parent – it is possible to consider the various options within the context of *eight* basic cases.

The way the calculation of maintenance is approached will vary from case to case, so we will take them as they come. The principles in Cases 3 and 4 below can be used to decide the global maximum available for the children whether or not any maintenance is payable between the parents. It may not be if the parent with the children has remarried, if the parents have themselves had a clean break on maintenance, or if the parents were never married. But if maintenance is being considered for children alone it would not now seem appropriate for any such maintenance to be allowed unless – and to the extent that – maintenance calculated under Cases 3 and 4 below exceeds the amount of any Child Support payable.

Case 1: One spouse has income, the other spouse has none, and there are no dependent children

For more than two centuries the courts have tended to say that, in this case, the spouse with income should pay one-third of his (now also possibly her) income as maintenance to the other.[1] In some cases they have talked about a 'one-third rule';[2] in others they have denied that there is a 'one-third rule'; but generally one-third is what they have aimed for, and in the average case the one-third principle is the one most commonly used and is the guide suggested in this case.

Why one-third? The payer will be earning the income and will have the expense and hassle of doing it; and, from the payer's point of view at least, the recipient merely has to sit at home and enjoy the maintenance received. Giving any more would be likely to inflame feelings of injustice and that would invite default and defeat the whole object of the exercise.

Case 2: Both spouses have income, one has more than the other, and there are no dependent children

Historically this case was dealt with by a crude extension of the one-third principle. The incomes of the two spouses were added together, the total was divided by three to produce one-third of their joint incomes, and the income of the spouse with the smaller income was deducted from that third. Anything left was maintenance.

But there was a snag in that for it meant that the recipient of maintenance gained no advantage by working until her (or his) income exceeded a third of the joint income; and after that the recipient received nothing.

This shows up starkly when the percentages are plotted on a graph (see Figure 1). For simplicity, Figure 1 assumes that the wife will be the recipient and the husband the payer, although that may be reversed if she has the higher income. In Figure 1 the horizontal axis takes the possible range – from 0 to 100 per cent – of the wife's income as a percentage of joint income. The vertical axis takes the possible range – again from 0 to 100 per cent – of the wife's income *plus maintenance* as a percentage of joint income. The line A–B shows how income plus maintenance stays flat at one-third of joint income whatever the maintained partner contributes; and how maintenance ends once that contribution (the dotted line) exceeds one-third.

Clearly what is needed is a way of scaling maintenance so that the recipient obtains some benefit for earning more, and has some incentive to do so. This is in everyone's interest, including the payer's.

Using the same graph it is possible to produce such a scale. We know from Case 1 that if the recipient has no income, the general approach would be that the payer should pay one-third of his income as maintenance. We know too that once the spouses' incomes are equal

Figure 1: *Wife produces less than 50 per cent of income – no children*

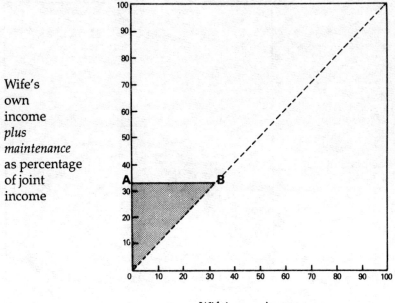

Wife's own income *plus maintenance* as percentage of joint income

Wife's own income
as percentage of joint income

there is no reasonable basis for maintenance of substance between them. So if the line defining the percentage of income including maintenance in Figure 1 were changed so that it runs from 33 per cent when the wife has no income to 50 per cent when she is producing 50 per cent herself, a scale emerges which allows all the intermediate percentages to be read off – line A–B in Figure 2.

So, for example, using Figure 2, if the wife is producing 30 per cent of joint income, she should have just under 42 per cent of joint income and 12 per cent of joint income will be her maintenance.

There is no legal authority for calculating maintenance this way, and no other authority except the logic advanced in this chapter. If you want to fight about it, you may get away, or be stuck, with the straight one-third approach or with some unpredictable modification of it. Otherwise, you may find it helpful to use Figure 2 as a guide if your circumstances bring you within Case 2. Appendix 3 spells out how you can apply the graph (and the others which follow) to your own circumstances.

Figure 2: *Wife produces less than 50 per cent of income – no children (alternative)*

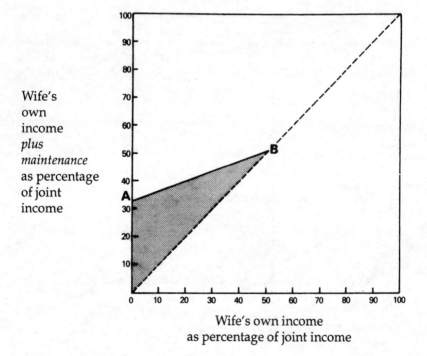

Wife's own income *plus maintenance* as percentage of joint income

Wife's own income as percentage of joint income

Case 3: There are dependent children in the care of a parent who has less than half of the parent's joint income

This has probably always been the commonest case in real life. But now the courts only consider it after Child Support has been assessed – and this case is only relevant in the courts if significant differences remain between the incomes of Parents with Care and Absent Parents *after* they have been adjusted for Child Support and the other factors referred to in Chapter 5.

If such differences do remain maintenance for the Parent with Care can anyway be considered under Case 2. But how might we introduce some precision into calculating what might be separately appropriate for children – on top of Parent with Care maintenance, if payable?

We know that if the parent with the care of the children had no income, a court would be most unlikely to order the other to pay more than 50 per cent of his or her income for all of them. To order any more would invite default which, for the reasons discussed in the introduction to this chapter, has always concentrated the minds of the courts. That therefore identifies a *maximum* amount of joint income which can be provided for the children at that extreme. For if the parent should, actually or notionally, have one-third (see Case 1) and overall they have a maximum of 50 per cent, 17 per cent is the *maximum* which can be provided for the children – however many there are and whatever ages they may be.

If we then go to the other extreme – where the parent's incomes are equal and nominal maintenance is the most that would be payable between them – another principle helps to define the margin. Basically, either parent may be ordered to pay maintenance for his or her children[3] so all other things being equal, they are equally liable. If, therefore, the maximum margin for child maintenance is 17 per cent of the payer's income when the other parent has none, the maximum ought to be half of that – 8.5 per cent – when the parents' incomes are equal.

These extremes allow us to place another line on the graph in Figure 2 to define the maximum percentage of joint income which may be awarded in child maintenance, on top of actual or notional maintenance for the parent. Figure 3 shows the result, and the line C–D identifies the maximum for child maintenance. Where the income of the parent with care of the children lies between 0 and 50 per cent of joint income, the maximum percentage for the children can be established by deducting the actual or notional percentage for the parent on line A–B from the percentage above it on line C–D.

That line, however, gives the maximum available for all children, whatever age they may be. Reasonably, the maximum is only likely

Figure 3: *Wife produces less than 50 per cent of income – children in her care*

Wife's
own
income
plus
(a)
wife's
maintenance
(b)
maximum
available
for
children as
percentage
of joint
income

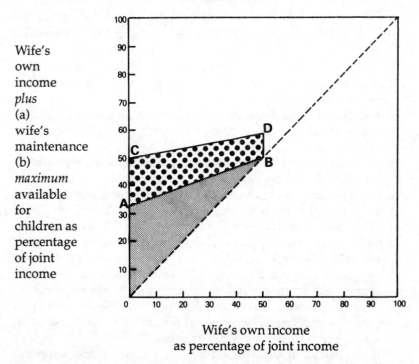

Wife's own income
as percentage of joint income

to be payable when the children are advancing in their teens. The question of how much of that maximum should actually be *paid* is dealt with under Case 8 below.

Remember the caution given about the use of Figure 2 at the end of the discussion of Case 2. It applies equally to Figure 3. Again, if you wish to use Figure 3, Appendix 3 describes how to apply it to your own circumstances. Remember also (as noted on page 86) that if maintenance is calculated for children alone under these principles it may not be appropriate to agree or order its payment save to the extent that that maintenance exceeds any Child Support payable.

Case 4: There are dependent children in the care of a parent who has more than half of the parents' joint income

In the fairly rare case where a parent with the care of children already has more than half of the parents' joint income, it clearly becomes more difficult to argue for any maintenance payment from the other on the basis of the principles which the courts apply. There is no real basis for any payment between the parents. But because both are liable to maintain their children there may still – up to a point – be a margin where the payment of some maintenance for the children by the parent with the lower income is appropriate.

No decision is known where any court has specifically concerned itself with this problem but one might suggest, as a rough guideline, that:

(a) some maintenance for children may still be appropriate when the parent with their care is producing between 50 and 60 per cent of joint income

(b) once the parent who has care of the children is producing more than 60 per cent of joint income, no more than a nominal order for the children – say 5p per annum – would be reasonable.

That, incidentally, ties in with the suggestions implicit in the graphs already referred to. For if the line C–D defining the maximum available for children in Figure 3 is projected (see Figure 4) it intersects

Figure 4: *Wife produces more than 50 per cent of income – children in her care*

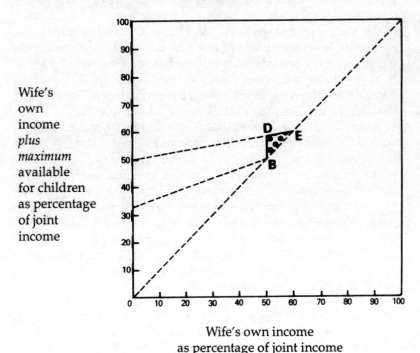

Wife's own income *plus maximum* available for children as percentage of joint income

Wife's own income as percentage of joint income

(at point E) with the dotted line representing the recipient's own income when that income reaches 60 per cent of the joint income. So, for example, if a recipient's income is 55 per cent of the whole, 59 per cent is the maximum of joint income to include child maintenance and 4 per cent is the maximum for such maintenance. Again any question of maintenance for children alone is subject to the caution given at the end of Case 3 above.

So, with the same qualifications as before, you may use Figure 4 to define the limits of child maintenance if your circumstances place you in Case 4. Again, Appendix 3 may help you to apply Figure 4 to your own circumstances.

Case 5: The reciprocal of Case 4: the position of the parent with the lower income where the other parent has care of children

While a parent with the lower income may still have to pay some maintenance for the children as discussed under Case 4, there must clearly come a point when the question arises of that parent – if the parties are or were married – *receiving* maintenance. Take, for example, the extreme case of someone with no income at all except perhaps means tested social security benefits. Perhaps he or she is totally disabled. A court has rejected a husband's argument for maintenance in one such case[4] but wives may fare better. Or consider the case of an Absent Parent with a very low percentage of the parties' joint income who still has to pay Child Support to a Parent with Care who has very substantial income – possibly with overall results which are bizarre. The courts might still redress the overall balance by ordering the Parent with Care to pay maintenance to the Absent Parent. It may be arguable that wives or husbands should receive maintenance in such cases – one-third of the other parent's income under Case 1 even if they have none. But if that is so, a final range may be defined on the principles already discussed. For it seems logical that the possible right of a spouse to *receive* maintenance should start when his or her income drops below the level at which he or she would cease to be liable to *pay* maintenance under Case 4. And if that is so, the range for him or her can be defined by adding a final line (E–F) to Figure 4 to produce Figure 5. On that basis, for example, a spouse producing 20 per cent of joint income would be entitled to maintenance giving him or her 38 per cent of joint income.

The previous warnings about the uses of the graph are repeated, but again Appendix 3 may help you to apply it to your own circumstances. There are no more versions of the graph to accompany

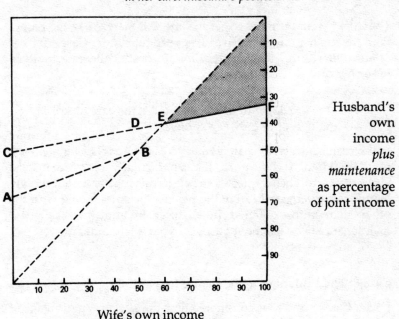

Figure 5: *Wife produces more than 60 per cent of income – children in her care: husband's position*

Husband's
own
income
plus
maintenance
as percentage
of joint income

Wife's own income
as percentage of joint income

the rest of the cases which can either be resolved by other methods or by reference to the methods already described.

Case 6: There are several children, some in the care of one parent and some in the care of the other

The position of new families is usually accommodated by adjusting the incomes of the parents before maintenance is calculated as suggested in Chapter 5. Here we are concerned with children of the same family.

It is rare for children in the same family to be split up (see Chapter 10) but it can happen. So, since this chapter attempts to consider all possible contingencies, we need to look at the possibility. Again, this is not easy, since no case is known in the law reports where any court has addressed itself specifically to the problem. But the simplest solution seems to be:

(a) to decide the maximum margin for maintenance for the children as if *all* the children were with the parent with the *lower* income – as under Case 3, and

(b) to decide what maintenance should actually be paid for each child – under Case 8 below.

Then the parent with the larger income will merely pay the parent with the smaller any maintenance appropriate under Case 3 for her or him, plus the maintenance appropriate for the children actually in his or her care.

Case 7: There are dependent children all in the care of third parties – maintenance between spouses

In this case, also rare, the parents may already be paying maintenance for the children to whoever has them, particularly if they are in local authority care. The simplest solution in this case is to deduct any maintenance being paid from the parents' incomes (along with the other deductions detailed in Chapter 5) and then calculate maintenance between the spouses on what is left under Cases 1 or 2 as if there were no children.

Case 8: The amount of maintenance for children

Under Cases 3 and 4 we considered how the *maximum* percentage of joint income available for child maintenance may be arrived at. As already emphasised, the principles in Cases 3 and 4 can be used to decide the global maximum available for children whether or not any maintenance is in fact payable between the parents. It may not be if the parent with the children has remarried, if the parents have themselves had a clean break on maintenance, or if the parents were never married.

If a child is disabled in any significant way, maintenance for that child may require special consideration. Otherwise, however, the age of the child or children is really the only variable to which significance can be attached.

From Cases 3 and 4 we derive a maximum possible provision for the children, however many there may be and whatever ages they may be. But obviously the maximum should only be payable when the children's needs are at their maximum. Common sense suggests that this is when they are in their teenage years and this seems to be the assumption when the courts consider child maintenance, although again no case is known where it has been specifically discussed.

How then may parents who wish to agree figures arrive at them? The cost of children in ordinary life normally rises by stages related to their age. As a suggestion, and it is no more than that for there are certainly no rules:

1. Stage 1 runs from birth to age 5 – when they start at primary school.
2. Stage 2 runs from 5 to 10 – most of their primary schooling.
3. Stage 3 runs from 10 to 13 – the start of secondary school and the early teens.
4. Stage 4 runs from 13 to 17 – secondary schooling and the middle teens.

If a child stays on in full-time education after 17, there may be a final stage – Stage 5 – running from 17 to whenever the child finishes in full-time education.

On this basis maximum maintenance should only be paid when the child or children are at Stage 4 or 5. But since Stage 5, if it happens at all, only comes in as a special 'extension' application for child maintenance, we will deal with the problem of calculation first on the basis that the first four stages only are relevant.

How then, starting with the maximum figure for maintenance derived from Case 3 or 4, may figures be calculated for each child?

The stages roughly reflect the way the cost of keeping children rises: £1 in Stage 1 becomes £2 in Stage 2, £3 in Stage 3 and £4 in Stage 4. So, as a very rough guide to calculating actual maintenance:

1. Divide the maximum amount for child maintenance calculated under Case 3 or 4 by the number of children to be maintained.
2. Allow one-quarter of the resulting figure for each child in Stage 1, one half for every child in Stage 2, three-quarters for every child in Stage 3, and the whole for each child in Stage 4.

If, then or subsequently, any child goes into Stage 5, substitute the following for the proportions set out in 2. above:

2. Allow one-fifth of the resulting figure for each child in Stage 1, two-fifths for every child in Stage 2, three-fifths for each child in Stage 3, four-fifths for each child in Stage 4 and the whole for each child in Stage 5.

This suggestion, like many others in this chapter, is offered in the hope that it will help those who wish to agree. It has no pedigree save the logic which is set out for it. It is, however, not likely to produce results which differ materially from those with which parents might end up if they battled it out through their lawyers and the courts.

The poor

We now come to the way in which maintenance calculated on the basis described for average families may be limited in the case of poor families. Here there are two classes of case:

1. *Subsistence level families* – where the potential payer of maintenance is either receiving DSS Income Support or Family Support, or his or her income is at or below the level of such support and the potential recipient is in much the same position.
2. *Marginal families* – where the income of the potential payer of maintenance, or the combined incomes of both parties, lies somewhere between DSS Income Support or Family Support levels and the average non-manual national wage (£18,174 gross in 1994) when an order for maintenance calculated on an average basis may reduce the income of the payer down towards or below subsistence level.

We will deal with these separately.

1. Subsistence level families

It has long been argued that if the potential payer has only subsistence income, there really is no scope for any maintenance order of substance which will not be punitive – and it is no part of modern law to punish. The essence of modern law is to compensate whichever spouse and children might otherwise lose out as a result of the breakdown of their relationship, to the extent that either spouse has resources with which such compensation can be achieved. Quite clearly, a spouse or parent with an income at Income or Family Support levels does not have such resources: these levels are designed to allow no more than the bare essentials of subsistence, and money which is tailored to those cannot possibly include enough to maintain anyone else.

This view was expressed in the Finer Report[5] and has been followed by the courts in several cases.[6]

Again, however, there is no hard-and-fast rule. There have been cases where people living on supplementary benefit (the equivalent of Income Support before 1988) have still been ordered to pay more than nominal (usually 5p a year) maintenance. In one such case the Court of Appeal said:

'In many, perhaps the majority of cases, the amount of supplementary benefit received would be the appropriate amount to satisfy his [the husband's] needs and enable him to be just above subsistence level. However, those rates were not to be blindly applied and in the present case there had been evidence which justified the making of the very modest order in respect of each child – £1 a week for each of three children.[7]

That logic was not very realistic. Obtaining the appeal decision probably cost the Legal Aid Fund the equivalent of 10, 15 or more years' maintenance at £3 a week, however much it might have gratified the parent caring for the children. Under the 1991 Child Support Act parents who are living on Income or Family Support and are fit and capable of work automatically have 5 per cent of their benefit deducted towards Child Support. But there does not seem to be any reasonable basis for the courts to make maintenance orders above nominal levels against such people.

2. *Marginal families*

The formulae and principles for calculating child maintenance under the 1991 Child Support Act are such that there is not likely to be any scope for the courts to order additional maintenance of substance in families where Child Support is payable. Child Support is geared to DSS allowances and principles and the courts themselves often applied those allowances and principles to the calculation of maintenance for marginal families before the Child Support Agency was set up.

Otherwise, the approach which the higher courts have tended to adopt with low income families has been simply to award as maintenance 50 per cent of the net income left after a wider range of deductions has been made under the 'net effect' approach (see Chapter 5, pages 71–7).[8] That approach is still likely to be followed when considering maintenance in cases where Child Support is not payable – for example, spousal maintenance when both spouses have low incomes.

The rich

The concept of maintenance as compensation appears early in the history of maintenance for the rich. As previously mentioned, courts have long indicated that maintenance should not be fixed at levels which exceed those which will allow recipients to maintain the standards of living which they enjoyed before maintenance; or the standards of living which, in the case of married people, they should have enjoyed if their spouse had not been excessively mean! The case of the rich is the one case in maintenance calculation where the previous standard of living may have any real relevance.

So, if you add up everything which you (or your partner) need to pay to continue your previous standard and style of living, and the end result is *less* than the amount of maintenance calculated on incomes under the earlier sections of this chapter for an average family, the total annual cost of your previous standard of living is likely to define the maximum amount of annual maintenance.

Of course, if you, or your spouse or former spouse, are rich, there will probably be resources available to fund a clean break which includes full compensation for abandoning maintenance for the spouse. But remember that the right to child maintenance cannot be compromised away; and clean break settlements between spouses must take account of Child Support payable under the 1991 Act – not least because Child Support includes support for the spouse living with the children.

Variation of the amount of maintenance

We dealt with the duration of the obligation to pay maintenance in Chapter 5, and we consider in detail the mechanics of how that obligation may be ended in a clean break in Chapter 8.

So long as any obligation to pay maintenance continues, however, the amount payable may be varied – up or down – at any time if the circumstances of either party have changed since the amount was last fixed by a court.

On any application to vary an order a court will balance the circumstances as they stood when the existing amount was fixed against the new circumstances. So it is usually important to keep records of the financial positions each time the court does consider amounts, particularly as applications to vary maintenance may be made years after the original order was made.

If a significant change can be shown in incomes, or perhaps in available incomes where a person has acquired a new partner, a court is likely to recalculate maintenance on the basis of the new circumstances and, if the recalculation indicates a decrease or increase, to make a corresponding order.

If the change is not financial as such – for example, there has been no change in incomes but the children are older and are inevitably costing more – a court might order a change if the margin of joint income available for child as opposed to spouse maintenance was not fully used up by the previous order. But Child Support payable under the 1991 Child Support Act is reviewed and, if appropriate, varied automatically by the Child Support Agency every two years.

Otherwise, where the incomes are unchanged, and the cake capable of division has not changed, only the most extreme changes in other circumstances are likely to make any difference.

On a variation application a court may also impose a clean break time-limit on the duration of the order if it is then satisfied that the recipient, after the defined date, should be capable of being self-supporting.

Essentially, therefore, if you are considering, or having to consider, any question of a variation, recalculating from the start on the principles set out in this and the previous chapter may give you an idea whether such variation is appropriate and, if so, what its amount might be.

Application to vary orders are made to the court which made the order or to the court currently responsible for its enforcement. It is, for example, possible to transfer county orders to magistrates courts (and vice versa) for enforcement, although they can be transferred back again if the original court is preferred for a variation application.

Conclusions on maintenance

This chapter has been concerned with the calculation of maintenance. The suggestions made take the limited number of precise guidelines which the courts have actually discussed over the years, and evolve them as is described in the light of:

(a) general practice
(b) the external limits which can be deduced from the precise guidelines and general practice
(c) the very precise rules for child maintenance effective under the 1991 Child Support Act.

The suggestions made concentrate almost exclusively on one component only of the multitude of factors in Section 25 to which a court is required to 'have regard' – the incomes of the parties. But in the case of the vast majority of average and below average families it is unrealistic to look at any of the other factors. For there is no way in which the total income which previously supported a given standard of living for one family can be divided so as to maintain as high a living standard for two. It has to be a carve-up.

Notes

1. *Cooke* v *Cooke* (1812) 2 Phillim 40
2. *Furniss* v *Furniss* (1981) *The Times* 29 October
3. Section 11B Guardianship of Minors Act 1971
4. *Seaton* v *Seaton* (1986) *The Times* 24 February
5. The Finer Report (1974) HM Stationery Office, Cmnd 5629: see *Shallow* v *Shallow* (1979) Fam 1
6. For example, *Williams* v *Williams* (1974) Fam 55; *Chase* v *Chase* (1982) *The Times* 24 October
7. *Freeman* v *Swatridge* (1984) *The Times* 18 April
8. *Stockford* v *Stockford* (1981) 12 Family Law

Chapter 7

Sharing Capital and Property

Introduction

In this chapter the word 'property' is used generally to describe any sort of property – houses, land, shares, savings, pension rights, inheritance rights and so on. As emphasised in Chapter 5, if any question arises of giving a specific proportion of the *value* of property, net values which allow for any tax or costs payable on realisation must be used for the purpose of calculation.

In 1993, in a Scottish case, a husband was ordered to transfer the matrimonial home to his wife subject to her paying him half its value.[1] In that case the House of Lords ruled that the property should be valued as at the date they separated and that is likely to be the general rule in cases involving spouses. But court orders may imply or stipulate later dates – for example, the date of the order or the date when the relevant share has to be paid, if that date is postponed for some considerable time.

The basic guidelines for determining what rights spouses and children may have to share in property are essentially the same. But the court's powers to award property rights to children are restricted to provision 'for the welfare, while a minor, of any child of the family who has not attained the age of 18'.[2] The parents of children may consent to property settlements on them which are more generous. But in the absence of consent the courts are not likely to order a property settlement which automatically benefits children beyond the age of majority.

The courts have wide powers to vary existing property arrangements between spouses. As a result, and again in the absence of consent between the parties, separate property settlements on their children are rare. The position of the children of married couples is usually assumed to be covered by the arrangements made between their parents. But the courts have no comparable power to vary the property rights of unmarried couples. In consequence they are showing an increasing willingness to order settlements in favour of the children of such couples since the question of whether children's parents were married does not affect *their* rights.[3] But the courts can only make such orders against the *parents* of children of unmarried relationships. If people merely live together they do not incur obligations for step-children accepted as members of their family as they may do if they marry.[4]

If relationships founder there are therefore significant differences between the property rights of:

1. Spouses.
2. Children.
3. Cohabitees.

Accordingly we will consider them separately and in that order.

Spouses

English principles and Scottish law

You will already know from Chapter 4 that the law governing property is the same as that governing maintenance – there are general principles to which the courts are required to 'have regard' and no more. In the relatively short period since that law has been in force there have been many reported court decisions on property issues, and it is extremely difficult to discover any consistent logic in most of them. Only in the small number of cases where spouses have owned a great deal of property is it possible for the courts to wheel and deal with property. Only in those cases does a general sharing philosophy emerge.

Mostly parties have only one or two significant assets – their houses, their family business or something of that nature. The art of the possible in those cases is frequently limited by the nature of the assets themselves. And quite clearly the courts are developing principles for dealing with particular types of asset which owe more to the problems created by the nature of the asset than to any general idea of fair or any other shares. So if you are concerned about the share you might receive in your family house, very different principles may apply from those which operate on your family business.

Life would be a lot easier for all of us if English law followed Scottish law. Recognising the turmoil which principles similar to the English ones had caused, Scotland established firm property guidelines in 1985.[5]

In Scotland there is a clear distinction between 'matrimonial property' and the rest, and only matrimonial property is divisible. Matrimonial property does not include anything which either of the spouses received individually by gift or inheritance. Nor does it include anything which the parties owned before the marriage, or acquired after they finally separated *except* a house and any contents of a house bought for the marriage.

So matrimonial property in Scotland is effectively what the spouses themselves put together during their marriage (including any proportion of pension rights created during the marriage) plus any house and its contents acquired before the marriage and intended as the future matrimonial home. The spouses keep what came to them individually outside the scope of matrimonial property. Only matrimonial property is shared.

The basic principle for sharing matrimonial property in Scotland is that it is shared equally. However, that proportion may change in special circumstances which may include:

(a) any prior agreement over ownership – an agreed settlement before marriage may have no effect whatever in English law but it may do in Scotland

(b) the source of the funds used to buy matrimonial property if they did not come from the spouse's own income and efforts – so if property owned before marriage is sold and other property is bought to replace it, the replacement may not automatically fall for division

(c) any dissipation of assets by either spouse: if one spouse has spent some of the matrimonial property, he or she may not then be entitled to come back and claim half of what's left

(d) the nature of the property and the extent to which it is reasonable to expect it to be realised, divided or used as security

(e) the expenses of valuation of transfer of property in the divorce – ie values must be looked at net of the cost of disposal or transfer.

Many of the principles now explicit in Scottish law can be found in specific English decisions. The difficulty is that there are often other decisions which point in the opposite direction. For example, in one case the English Court of Appeal said that one of the reasons for giving a wife the large proportion of a farm was that it had been given to her by her father.[6] In Scotland that farm would not now be an asset to be shared because it would not be matrimonial property. But in another English case, decided two years earlier, the court said that the husband's prospect of becoming entitled to a large amount of money under a family settlement should be taken into account and a lump sum order of £30,000 to the wife was doubled for that reason. Similarly a husband has benefited from a wife's overseas trusts.[7] There are, however, *some* limits. Where a wife was tenant of a house owned by her mother, and might eventually inherit the house when her mother died, the court refused a husband's application to leave open his claim to share in what the wife might inherit when the mother died.[8]

English courts have decided that a man should keep the house entirely when he owned it before the marriage took place[9] but that was also a case where the marriage was of short duration and the principle that material financial provision is not appropriate in such cases also entered into the decision.

Certain principles are common in both Scottish law and English practice. For example, English courts consider that pension rights should be taken into account[10] although they have not specifically limited the principle to the value of those rights which has arisen during the marriage; and English courts have also used the principle that a party must account for assets which he or she has dissipated.[11] One way of dealing with the latter problem is to decide what the spouse who dissipated them received (eg if he or she sold shares and went on a binge with the proceeds) and then treat that as part of his or her share.

The advantage of Scottish law is that it eliminates beyond any doubt any question of sharing property which people owned before they married or received by gift or inheritance from their family. The idea that someone should have to share property which they accumulated before they married – through their own effort or in a previous marriage – or property which came to them by personal family gifts or inheritance, is one of the most bitterly felt, bitterly resented and bitterly fought. The English courts may or may not exclude such property in whole or in part from being shared, but the chances are that if you or your spouse have property which would not be liable to be shared at all in Scotland, and wish to avoid a costly battle, you may better serve both your interests by carving up what you have on the principles of Scottish law, rather than guesswork as to what an English court may do.

So far as property in general is concerned we have already identified a distinction between the cases where the spouses have a good deal of property and the courts can wheel and deal with it and the more common case where the parties have only one or two significant assets and the nature of the assets themselves limits what can be done. We will look first, therefore, at the position of the rich – people with considerable property in different forms – and then at the position of the majority whose concern is likely to be with particular types of property only.

The rich

Wealth reduces practical problems. It may not make spouses any happier when their relationships founder, but at least they can both expect to endure their unhappiness in comfort. Where assets are reasonably easy to divide there has been a tendency to follow the one-third principle – ie the spouse with the greater share should not be required to transfer more assets than suffice to leave the other with one-third of the total in value.[12, 13] But the time-honoured principle in maintenance that financial provision should not exceed that necessary to sustain the standard of living which a spouse had, or should have had, in marriage has also been imported into property provision. The courts have said:

> 'On the true construction of Section 25 there comes a point, in cases where the available resources are very large, when the amount required to fulfil its terms "level off" and redistribution of capital, in some unspecified ratio, begins which is outside the section.'[14]

Yet the scale of the possible differences in the treatment of property disputes still emerges starkly from the cases cited:

1. A 1981 case[15] involved a husband with assets worth £2.3 million who faced no problem in raising cash, a wife who only had a half share in the matrimonial home, and a marriage which had lasted for 23 years. The court ordered the husband to pay the wife £600,000 (ie approximately one-third) and the Court of Appeal did not consider that excessively high.
2. A 1983 case[16] involved a husband with assets worth £2.1 million. Again, the wife had virtually nothing. The parties had been married for 40 years, and both were then 67 years old. The husband's assets were largely locked up in a series of farms and the wife had worked all her life on them and had helped to build them up. However, selling more than a given proportion of the farms might disrupt the husband's business and threaten the livelihoods of his employees who included the spouses' four children. The court ordered the husband to pay the wife £375,000.

Even where very large values are concerned, the extent to which they can easily be realised or transferred may have a profound bearing on what emerges.

The majority

Most of us who have any wealth at all do not have it in cash, or in a form which can easily be reduced into cash. Unless there is some fluid wealth around, either to divide or to compensate for property which cannot easily be divided or transferred, the problems inherent in the property itself may dictate who can have what.

This problem is best considered by looking at the specific types of property which most commonly come into the reckoning.

1. *The family home*

Basic problems

The problems in sharing the spouses' former family home usually revolve around children and the need, if reasonable and possible, to keep them in it until they finish at school. First consideration has to be given to the children[17] but if they are to keep their home, there is no way in which it can be shared out until their need has passed.

Sometimes hard reality supervenes. For example:

(a) if the house is subject to a mortgage and the spouses' incomes are such that enough cannot be found by way of maintenance once they are divided to allow the spouse with the children to continue to pay the mortgage and other outgoings, the house has to be sold and what's left divided

(b) if, at the other extreme, the house is extremely valuable – sufficient, if sold, to buy a house for each half of the divided family – sale and division of the proceeds of sale is the most likely end result, particularly if the size of the house is excessive for both of the divided halves of the family, and it has no assets of significance apart from the house

(c) if there are no dependent children and no other significant assets, again the house may be sold and its proceeds divided between the spouses.

There may also be problems if someone else shares the house – the granny flat is a typical example. If granny has a specific, self-contained flat to which she has a formal title as owner or leaseholder (and whether the spouses gave it to her by deed of gift or she paid for it) she is like any owner of property, and the house can only be sold – if sale is otherwise appropriate – subject to her right to stay if she wishes. The same applies if she is a tenant protected by the Rent Acts.

If, however, she merely shares use of the house, she is like any other cohabitee. If she has contributed to the cost of the house, or is named on the deeds of the property as a co-owner, she will have a right to share in the proceeds of sale if the property is sold (cohabitees' rights are dealt with later in this chapter).

Otherwise the fact that she is there is not likely to have any bearing on whether or not the property should be sold. If sale is appropriate apart from her presence, then sale is still likely to be ordered if it cannot be agreed. The spouses' rights are not altered merely because one of them has granny living with them.

Sale of the home may present its own problems, particularly if the proceeds of sale, however divided, are not enough to buy any replacement. But the real problems arise when the divided incomes of the spouses are enough, but often only just enough, to make it possible to keep the house going for one of the spouses, with or without children. We will consider that position – which is very common – in detail.

Parent stays on in the home with children

A court may well order that the spouse who has the children shall continue to have use of the house and its contents, at least until the children reach the age of 17. If it does, the order may provide that the house shall then be sold and the proceeds of sale divided in defined proportions between the spouses. The same principle has been followed in allowing a wife to retain the matrimonial home indefinitely during her life so long as she does not remarry or have a man living with her. Orders such as this have also been used when it has not been possible to provide what the court regards as enough out of the free resources of the spouses. So, for example, in a case involving a man of 64 and a wife of 45, the man had stayed on in the matrimonial home and had provided another home for the wife when they separated. However, the value of the spouses' assets overall were such that there was little apart from the two houses out of which any provision could be made for the wife – £2,500 by way of lump sum order. So the court ordered that when the husband sold his house or died the wife should, in addition, have 20 per cent of the proceeds of his house. However, the court rejected the idea that it should put a definite end date on the wife's right: originally, the husband had been ordered to pay the 20 per cent anyway when he reached 70 years of age.[18]

Orders under which one spouses's rights are deferred like this used to be very common. They became known as *Mesher or Martin orders* after the cases in which their use was first reported.[19] But then Mesher and Martin orders fell out of fashion. They were criticised as offending the clean break ideal; and because spouses who retained use of the home often faced real hardship when the carve-up came and they had to find somewhere else to live. Yet the difficulty was and is that the only answer to that is to give the whole house to the spouse who is allowed to live in it. And that is often very harsh on the other. Now the pendulum is beginning to swing back again. In 1990 the Court of Appeal ruled that Mesher or Martin orders are still justified in appropriate cases.[20]

It will, however, always be the case that Mesher and Martin orders lead to a minefield of problems, and the position goes from bad to worse if these problems are not anticipated in the terms of the order – as all too often has been the case.

The basic circumstances in which a Mesher or Martin order may be made have already been identified sufficiently to allow you to recognise whether such an order is likely in your case, and whether it may save costs and dispute to agree to a settlement on the Mesher or Martin basis. So to complete the picture we now look at the problems which the order should also cover. In speaking of them we shall assume that the wife is remaining in the family home and the husband is leaving it, but the same circumstances may arise in reverse. Whichever way it is, however, the problems must all be considered before any decision can be reached as to whether your divided incomes in fact make it possible for the home to be retained.

Problems in Mesher and Martin orders

(a) Mortgage repayments

Mortgage interest arising on mortgages, or the proportion of mortgages up to £30,000 value, is allowed against tax. During marriage husband and wife count as one person so they only have one allowance of £30,000 between the two of them. After they separate each may be entitled to an allowance of £30,000 but, since the Finance Act 1988, only against different houses. So if the wife, and usually children, are to stay on in the matrimonial home, it is usually important to make sure that the mortgage on that home is payable by her out of her income. Then she can claim mortgage interest tax relief on any mortgage on that home up to £30,000 and her husband is free to acquire another mortgage on another home for himself and obtain tax relief against his income on that home. In cases where Mesher and Martin orders are involved that is often the only way he can hope to be able to buy another home.

If the matrimonial home is already in joint names, both spouses are jointly liable on the mortgage anyway and all that may need to be done is for the wife to make the payments. If it is not, it may be necessary for it to be put in joint names with the consent of the building society. Alternatively, the property and the mortgage may be transferred into the name of the wife alone, but dependent on the level of the wife's income the husband may then have to guarantee the wife's repayments.

If tax relief is given under the MIRAS scheme (Mortgage Interest Relief At Source) as is usually the case now, interest which qualifies for tax relief will be payable less tax anyway, and the relief will be given regardless of whether the payer has any taxable income out of which to pay it. Otherwise the change in the basis for taxation for maintenance brought about by the Finance Act 1988 may add another complication. MIRAS apart, the payer of mortgage interest can only recover mortgage interest tax relief if, and to the extent that, the payer has taxable income and is liable to tax on it. Maintenance payable under new maintenance orders (broadly those made after the 1988 Budget) will not be taxable income. So from now on only those who have taxable income apart from maintenance will be able to obtain any advantage from mortgage interest tax relief on mortgages which are not covered by MIRAS.

It is therefore important to make sure that housing arrangements which involve mortgages and mortgage interest tax relief are designed so as to keep alive both spouses' chances of obtaining full tax relief. Otherwise those who might have kept homes going before 1988 may not be able to do so. Any loss of tax relief inevitably means that spouses' incomes – and possible levels of maintenance – will be less.

(b) Repairs, insurance and other outgoings

Arrangements under which a spouse is to remain in occupation of the matrimonial home must take provision for the ongoing costs of running it. These are all costs which arise because the spouse in occupation and any children are to have continued use of the home and therefore form part of their maintenance costs. As with mortgages, if the wife's income out of divided resources does not suffice to cover these costs, the home cannot be retained.

(c) Ultimate sale and division of proceeds

If the property is ultimately to be sold and the proceeds then divided between the spouses, it is usual to provide that the net proceeds only should be divided. But the meaning of 'net proceeds' should be defined. There will be some costs when the property is sold – estate agents' and solicitors' charges, for example – and it is usual to provide that these shall be deducted from the proceeds of sale.

There may also still be a mortgage outstanding on the property, so it should also be stipulated that some part at least of any balance of the outstanding mortgage should be deducted. But how much? From the time the wife starts repaying the mortgage out of her income, any reduction of the mortgage debt will be made by her alone out of her separate income and resources. On basic principles it would not be right for her husband then to benefit by a proportion of that reduction. On the other hand, if the wife fails to pay the mortgage, arrears of capital and interest may arise. If the whole mortgage debt at the time of sale comes off the proceeds before they are divided, the husband will end up paying a proportion of those arrears, even though he has been paying maintenance out of which, typically in these cases, the mortgage repayments should have been made.

The answer to those problems is to provide that the amount of the mortgage debt at the time the original order is made should be deducted; and that if the mortgage at the time of sale is less – or more – than that amount, the wife should be paid – or should pay – the difference in full.

If the ultimate carve-up of the value of the property is based on the price which it realises when sold[21] the ultimate sum may include a substantial capital gain since the time of the order. Wives who have been in sole occupation and maintaining property and mortgages for years often consider it unjust that their former partner should also end up with a slice of any capital gain accrued over those years. But they should bear in mind that they had the use of their former husband's share locked up in the property over all those years and that it would not be right, when he finally receives it, that he should also lose any amount by which changes in values over the period may have increased the total value. After all, wives would not want him to be protected at their expense if values fell.

Husbands may, however, still face a tax problem on their share of any increase. The principal private dwellinghouse of individuals is at present free of Capital Gains Tax. But when the property is sold, it will no longer be the principal private dwellinghouse of the husband, and while there are some tax rules which may protect him he may be liable to Capital Gains Tax on any gain included in his share even if the wife is exempt by being in occupation.

Finally, Mesher and Martin orders inevitably presuppose that at some defined future date or event, the wife is going to find herself having to sell her home and to start again with only a proportion of the value of the house – when she will be older and possibly less well equipped to do it. She can, of course, negotiate, or attempt to negotiate, terms under which she will buy her husband's interest out and become sole owner of the property at any time; and she may well be able to persuade him to agree to that, and at a much reduced price if it is done long before her husband will otherwise receive his share.

But it is fairly common for Mesher and Martin orders also to include a right for her to buy out her husband's interest in any event at valuation when or before the question of sale would otherwise arise, although if the property is then still subject to mortgage, she will first have to obtain the consent of the building society or other lender to the transaction.

A court order for ultimate payment of defined shares in a house which takes account of all these factors might conclude with words something like these:

1. If, on or before the time when the property is to be sold and the proceeds distributed, the wife informs the husband in writing that she wishes to buy the property herself, then the property shall be valued by a valuer agreed between the parties (or failing agreement by a valuer nominated by the President for the time being of the Royal Institution of Chartered Surveyors on the application of either party) such valuer to act as expert and not as arbitrator. The value of the property so determined shall be treated as if it were the proceeds of sale of the property realised on sale of the property and, upon the wife paying to the husband his share of the net proceeds of sale calculated as set out below, the husband shall convey all his estate or interest in the property to her and she shall become its sole owner.

2. When the property is sold the proceeds of sale shall be applied in payment:
   (a) of legal and estate agents' charges of and incidental to sale
   (b) of any outstanding balance of the mortgage on the property existing at the date of this order
   (c) of any capital taxes payable if both spouses are liable to such taxes (but not any for which the husband alone is liable) on the sale of the property
   (d) to the wife of the amount (if any) by which the amount of the mortgage debt has been reduced from the amount of £   existing at the date of this order
   (e) to the husband of the amount (if any) by which the amount of the mortgage debt has been increased from the amount of £   existing at the date of this order

(f) of the balance to the spouses in the following shares:
- to the wife   X per cent
- to the husband   Y per cent

Who has what share in the home?

There are many cases, whether the home is sold immediately, or sale is deferred under a Mesher or Martin order, where the courts have ordered that the proceeds of sale shall be divided equally between the spouses.[22] But a spouse allowed to stay on in the home is now likely to end up with a greater share of its value so that he or she is better placed to acquire another house when the home has to be sold. Proportions of 60:40 per cent[23] and 62.5:37.5 per cent[24] have been awarded in favour of the spouse staying on in the home.

Application of the principle that shares in the home should be loaded against a spouse who has alternative accommodation is seen most clearly in those cases where the alternative already exists when the original order is made. For example, where a husband stayed on in the home and the wife remarried and had a new home with a man who was rich, the husband was given 92 per cent and the wife 8 per cent.[25]

So one might offer the following rough guidelines on defining the shares which spouses shall receive when the matrimonial home is the only significant asset, and its proceeds are to be divided:

(a) in immediate sale cases 50:50
(b) where the sale may not take place for some years (eg when the children are young and the spouse with their care may have to pay off substantial parts of the mortgage). Anything between 60 per cent and 100 per cent in favour of the spouse who stays on
(c) where the outgoing spouse is established in another home 75–100 per cent in favour of the spouse who stays on.

2. *The family business*

If a family business is to continue, any financial provision which can be carved out of it will depend on what the business can afford. And if the parties' assets, plus whatever can be found from the business, do not allow enough to achieve reasonable provision between them, the one who does not have the business has to be content with what can be achieved.

Only rarely do spouses who have failed to find enough harmony to make a go of a marriage find enough to go on working together harmoniously in a business. Usually one goes on running it and the other has to leave. But the one who leaves cannot then expect a share in the value of the business which will bankrupt it, destroying jobs and the only goose capable of laying golden eggs out of which maintenance may be paid.

Where families' livelihoods come from businesses – factories, farms, guesthouses, professional businesses, shops and so on – usually one of the spouses is the prime mover, and the other participates to a lesser degree, although in some cases both are equally involved. If the business is a professional business depending on professional qualifications and only one of the spouses has the required qualification, it will usually only survive if that spouse retains it. If, for example, the wife is a solicitor, dentist or chemist and the husband is not (or vice versa) the business has to stay with the spouse who has the qualification, unless it is convenient for it to be sold. But even if it does not require a specific qualification, it may have to stay with the spouse who effectively runs it.

The origin of the business may also play a part in this. Many businesses start off with the families of one or other of the spouses and are acquired by that spouse by family gift or inheritance and are therefore likely to stay with him or her. So, for example, where a wife's father gave her and her husband a farm, she kept the farm for herself and her children, and her husband, although he had worked on the farm throughout their marriage, went out.[26]

So the history and nature of the business may determine who stays with the business and who goes out.

Where the business includes several units each of which are, or can be, independent of one another, it may be possible for the husband to take some of the units and the wife to take others. This may be possible, for example, if the parties own several shops. It was possible in circumstances where the family owned a garage and a café – the husband kept the garage and the wife the café. In circumstances where the business can be carved up like this it is often possible to arrive at a broad equality between the property which each spouse ends up with and have a final deal between them with no ongoing commitments either way.

It is therefore possible to identify some tentative guidelines for businesses:

If the business is to continue

(a) if the business came from the family of one of the spouses, usually that spouse keeps the business

(b) if it did not (and occasionally this is the only practical solution even if it did) the business stays with a spouse who in large proportion has been involved in running it, particularly if his or her professional qualifications make him or her the only spouse who can continue to do so

(c) if the business is divisible and both spouses have been running it, or each spouse could run a divided part of it, dividing the business between them is likely to be the solution

(d) very occasionally the spouses find they can continue to work together. In that event they are likely to go on as before.

Resolving the future of a continuing business also resolves who will have the income from it for purposes of maintenance calculation under the previous chapter.

Shares in a continuing business

But what share of a continuing business may a spouse expect if the business and its value are to stay with the other spouse? As a going concern the business may be very valuable, but that value often exists only on paper unless or until it is sold. It is not in the nature of any successful business to hold large sums of cash or substantial assets which are not required to keep it going and which can be handed over to an outgoing spouse. And if anyone tried to carve large sums of money out of it, that may wreck the business, destroy jobs and destroy incomes which are often the only basis for maintenance. Moreover, if the marriage had continued, neither spouse would have been able to lay hands on the value of the business anyway.

Inevitably, the courts have had to face this problem and the answers they have produced for spouses going out of a business have been pretty bleak. They have said effectively that whatever the business may be worth on paper, an outgoing spouse can only expect to receive such a sum as the business can reasonably raise without imperilling its future existence. So, where the wife retained a farm then worth £102,000 which her father had given her, her husband, then 44, who had worked the farm throughout the marriage, and had no qualifications except those of a farm worker, received only £15,000 – which was all the wife could reasonably raise by borrowing.[27]

In reaching this decision the court added cold comfort for others:

'If we had been dealing here with something with which we are rather more familiar than farming, perhaps, say, a solicitor's practice, no one would have thought for a moment of suggesting that a solicitor should be called on to realise his share in a partnership in order to provide a lump sum of capital for his wife or former wife. Here it would be quite unreal to go beyond what is the limit of the practical.'

If the family has other property which does not involve difficulties in division, the full value of the business may be brought into the balance so that the spouse who keeps the business has that as his or her share or part of it, and the other spouse has a greater proportion of the free property. In that event they may end up with equal or more equal shares of the values – paper and real. But in many cases the most which they have outside the business is the home. Even that may be tied into the business by mortgages or other security obtained to support the business, and often – farms and guesthouses are an example – the home may be physically part of the business. Where they are separate, one spouse may receive the home and the other the business; we have already referred to a case where that happened.[28]

There is one other option in some cases.

Although it may not be possible to raise funds either directly or by borrowing out of a business, preserving its existing *facility* to borrow may not be so important as long as it does not give rise to any new borrowing cost. A dentist approaching retirement, for example, may be established with his surgery in his home; he may have to stay there to earn the income necessary to maintain himself and his wife; and it may not be in the interest of either of them to reduce that income by further borrowing even if it is possible. But it may be possible to agree that when he retires and the property is sold she shall have a share of the value then realised, and that share shall be secured by a charge – effectively a mortgage on which no interest is paid – on the property.

In such cases it may be possible to give the outgoing spouse a *future* right, secured by charge or mortgage on the business or on some of its property, which pays nothing immediately but something later, perhaps at some defined date, perhaps only when the business is sold. If that can be done, the outgoing spouse will at least then have a right to benefit from the value of the business as, and at the time when, he or she might have done had the marriage continued.

Arrangements as complicated as this can usually only be arrived at by prior negotiation and agreement and with the help of a solicitor. But the way they are approached is to consider the net value of the business if it were sold immediately – that is, the price it might fetch less all the costs and taxes which would be payable on sale – and the *percentage* of that net value which the outgoing spouse would then be entitled to.

The outgoing spouse then obtains an order that in defined future circumstances – sale of the business, death of the other spouse, and possibly at a defined or ascertainable future date – the 'business' spouse will pay a lump sum equal to the determined percentage of the net value or net proceeds of sale, the meaning of 'net' being defined, of course. Such an order will also provide that payment of the defined percentage shall be secured by a charge (or mortgage), usually in previously agreed terms, on the assets of the business or on certain defined assets. The charge will be a separate document which, typically, will include the right of the outgoing spouse to compel sale at the defined time.

Such charges restrict the extent to which a business spouse can borrow in the future, so they cannot be used where the business is likely to need that borrowing facility. But their advantages are that they do not impose any immediate cost on the business; they guarantee the outgoing spouse an interest in the value of the business when that value would normally be available to the business spouse; and they reduce the extent to which the spouses may have to make or receive compensating or balancing transfers of any other assets, or to do without. They also reduce outgoing spouses' sense of injustice, and the risk that, without such arrangements, they may feel that they have nothing to lose and may as well, regardless of costs, fight their case up through the courts to see if they can get anything better. Where the family businesses are involved, there are incentives for both spouses to contemplate such deals.

If the business is not to continue

The problems disappear if the business is not to continue. In that event it can be sold for whatever it will realise and the net proceeds, added to anything else the spouses have, will be divided between them.

3. Pension rights

Pensions are usually personal to the spouse whose employment funds them. If they are not divisible or transferable, they can be – and are – valued; but nothing can be done to compensate the other spouse for their value unless the pensionable spouse has other assets which can be transferred instead.

Pension rights are not wealth which is immediately available to the spouse who has them, and while they may in the end give that spouse lump sums of cash and income out of which he or she can continue to pay maintenance, circumstances may then have changed so radically that the other spouse will not gain any benefit. On the other hand, pension rights are a form of saving. The family's income and standard of living have been lower during the marriage because that saving has been made, and if pension payments are deducted before the spouses' incomes are calculated for maintenance purposes, maintenance will be lower and the spouse receiving maintenance will, therefore, continue effectively to contribute to the accumulation of pension rights. Finally, the pension rights of one spouse will usually guarantee a pension to the other if he or she survives and the right to that pension will be lost if divorce ends the marriage.

It is possible for a qualified actuary, and usually for the managers of existing pension funds, to value pension rights as they exist at a given date. The basic value is discounted to allow for the period still to elapse before the pension actually becomes payable and the accidents along the way which may prevent it being paid. It is also possible for insurance and other similar companies which offer annuities and pension schemes to quote the cost of buying a pension to replace any existing rights which a spouse will lose on divorce.

Where the general resources of the spouses are sufficient, the discounted value of existing pension rights may be included in the cash value of the assets which they possess, and the one who does not have the rights may as a result receive a higher proportion of other property by way of compensation. Again, where resources are sufficient, financial provision may include the purchase of a pension by the spouse who has pension rights for a spouse who will lose such rights through divorce.

But it must be emphasised that these things are only possible where the family has sufficient resources at the time the marriage breaks down to allow for such compensation. Not much can be done if all they have is a house, its contents and their incomes, although if the house after mortgage has some value, a 'larger' share in the value of the house for the spouse who loses out in the pension field may be appropriate. Unless spouses have ample free resources it is unlikely that enough will be available to take on board the full value of pension rights, or even to justify the cost of having them valued.

4. *The contents of the home – including cars*

If the existing home is to be maintained for children, they will probably need to go on using the existing contents, and failing all else a Mesher order may even include an order to that effect. The outgoing spouse may have to leave behind virtually everything which the children will need, and very little may survive or have any value by the time the house is sold.

Where children are not involved decisions may have to be made as to who shall have what. Relative to other parts of the property conundrum, this may generate an utterly disproportionate cost and delay if the spouses cannot themselves agree. And even going to court to fight out claims over contents may be entirely impractical. Often the likely costs exceed even the value of the contents, and legal aid will not be granted for such claims. This is a particular hardship for spouses who lived in a rented home where the contents are virtually all they have. They may have to put up with whatever each of them manages to grab if they cannot agree.

Attempting to divide a family's furniture, fixtures, fittings, equipment and car or cars is an almost intractable problem if the spouses cannot themselves agree what should be done.

A court can order that everything be sold so that the cash can be divided, but that is rare, not least because it entails a massive loss of resources to the family – second-hand values are a derisory proportion of the cost of acquisition. Alternately it can, at great cost, order the parties – or even a surveyor – to prepare lists of all the contents. In theory it can go through those lists and order who shall have what. But in reality the law does not offer any adequate solution to contents disputes unless the contents are worth so many thousands of pounds that there will still be something worthwhile left after costs.

All one can offer, therefore, are suggestions which may help you to agree a division of what you have:

1. Each of you should always have his or her own personal clothes and belongings.
2. If individual items were owned by either of you before you married or were given to you individually by your families or friends, it is realistic that you should have these if you want them.
3. If items are duplicated, and unless dividing them up destroys a major part of their value – it might with a matching pair of Ming vases – it is reasonable that each of you should have half of the duplicated items.
4. Everything else should be divided more or less equally, and if you cannot agree such division item by item, you might try a very old solution. One of you should prepare what you consider to be two equal lists, and the other should have first choice of list.
5. If you own one car only, and one of you has to use it for work, the

car should stay with the one who uses it for work. If you have two or more cars, each should stick with the one he or she mostly uses; any others should be sold, unless perhaps you have older children who usually have use of a car and both of you agree that they should benefit. If there are sufficient general resources of cash to allow for compensating payments, cars which are retained should be valued and the spouse retaining them should make such payments to the other as ensure that each is equal in value terms on the car account.

6. If anything which is yours under the above headings has to be left in the home for the benefit of the children, it should be identified and agreed that you may take possession of it when the children's need has ended.

Property in general

Insofar as property is free of any of the constraints which apply to homes, businesses, pension rights and contents already discussed – and it may become so if they have to be sold – the tendency is to use such free property to balance the shares of the spouses up towards equality and to achieve a 50:50 split of *net values* where this can be done. But with property in particular the court, if it goes that far, is likely to lay emphasis on the words of Section 25(2)(f)[29] which require it to have regard to 'the contributions which each of the parties has made . . . to the welfare of the family'.

So if most of the assets available for distribution came from outside the marriage, and particularly with short marriages, equality may not be what is aimed for: indeed, with short marriages no transfer of assets may arise at all.

But, as one must constantly emphasise, there are no hard rules or definable modes of practice. Generally:

1. If everything which you own is in cash, can easily be turned into cash, or has to be turned into cash, the chances are that a court will order a lump sum payment which leaves each of you with about half of that cash.
2. If your property includes a mixture of assets and there is no special problem with transferring some of them, a court may make lump sum or property transfer orders which collectively leave each of you with approximately half of the total net value.
3. Where problem assets dominate your financial position the limitations imposed by the nature of those assets may define what

you can have. If other assets do not allow enough to achieve broad equality, you will have to put up with whatever can be achieved.

Children

The courts' powers to make orders which *compel* parents to settle property on their children are only exercised rarely, though such orders are now more likely in the case of children of unmarried parents – for example, to ensure that they retain use of a home when that cannot be achieved by making an order against the relevant parent (see the introduction to this chapter, page 101).

One of the reasons for the rarity of such orders is that provision for children is essentially limited to questions of 'the welfare, *while a minor*, of any child of the family *who has not attained the age of 18*'.[30] The courts have no power to set children up for life, and any property provision intended for their welfare under 18 almost always goes in consequence to the spouse with their care.

It is, however, a fact of life that children who might ultimately have expected some portion of their parents' wealth in due course often lose out altogether if their parents divorce and then remarry or form new associations. Either or both may have more children from new relationships; and all too often whatever each of them emerges with from the divorce then passes on to their new partners and new children. Indeed, if a spouse remarries and then dies, the new spouse may inherit everything leaving the children in the cold.

So there is a case for including children in the carve-up by *consent* if parents have anything of substance, and that case arises particularly where the family home is to be retained by a parent because he or she has the care of the children and is retaining it for their benefit. For it may help to solve the problems of the carve-up, and the future problems of the spouse with care of the children, if the ultimate shares in the value of the house are split three ways:

1. One-third to mother.
2. One-third to father.
3. One-third to trustees for the children on terms that:
   (a) the children's third be left in the house until it is sold anyway, and
   (b) after that it remains available to help provide a house for the parent with the initial care of the children until he or she dies or remarries.

Apart from the obvious ultimate benefit to the children, a trust such as that, to which both parents contribute, may make the whole set-up of a Mesher arrangement more acceptable to both parents, and easier to agree as a result. The outgoing parent will not be faced with so large a share passing absolutely to the parent whose care of the children otherwise seems to carry a disproportionate financial advantage. And the parent who has the care of the children will not face so serious a problem in buying out the other parent, or finding a replacement home, if that parent has two-thirds of the value of the existing house available – one-third in his or her own right and another from the children's trust.

It is unlikely that you will be able to set up such trusts and avoid the tax pitfalls without advice and help from a solicitor. But if you are trying to save the cost of having separate lawyers *negotiate* an acceptable deal between you, it may help you to know that a children's settlement along these lines can be part of any package which you contemplate.

Cohabitees – the unmarried

General

The property rights of people who have lived together and then split up – and this goes for any people who live together, not merely those who live as man and wife – are far more restricted than those of people who are or were married. If cohabitees live out their joint lives together, the survivor may have more substantial claims on the estate of the first to die. Those rights, however, may also involve conflicting claims with surviving spouses and other dependants of the deceased. Logically, they fall to be considered in questions of wills and inheritance and so they are discussed more fully in Chapter 9.

Here we are concerned only with what happens if cohabitees' relationship founders while they are alive.

Temporary protection – domestic violence

First of all it should be noted that cohabitees, like spouses, can claim *temporary* protection for their occupation of property in the magistrates or County Courts if they are at risk of violence from their partner.[31] Indeed, a court can grant them an injunction or order excluding their partner, for a period at least, even from a house which he or she owns or of which he or she is the tenant.[32] But such an order will not change the ownership or tenancy rights in the property, and if the cohabitee so protected has no such rights, sooner or later he or she can be compelled to leave the home and the other cohabitee will then have it as his own. In addition, if there is no violence, a cohabitee cannot exclude his or her partner from the home if the partner is an owner, joint owner, tenant or joint tenant.[33]

Ownership rights – financial shares

Cohabitees will only have ownership rights of property of any sort – houses, land, furniture, cash, shares or anything else – if:

1. They owned it before the cohabitation started, acquired it in their own name out of their own funds during or after cohabitation ended, or received it as some personal gift or inheritance from a third party (*separate ownership*), or
2. It is owned jointly with a fellow cohabitee – with or without others (*joint ownership*), or
3. They have made a contribution in money or money's-worth towards the price of the property (*implied joint ownership*).
4. It was given to them by their partner as a Donatio Mortis Causa – when their partner was at point of death.[34]

As before we will deal with these issues separately.

1. *Separate ownership*

Gifts *from third parties* to one of the cohabitees will remain the property of the cohabitee to whom the gift was made. But if a cohabitee provides the funds with which his or her partner buys property in the partner's name, no gift is implied and what is known as a *resulting trust* arises. If there is no deed or document to make clear that a gift was intended, the cohabitee who provided the funds may in due course be able to recover the property. So, for example, when a Miss Crane gave a Mr Davis a cheque to buy property in his name, it was held that she could subsequently recover the property.[35] Equally, when a woman, who had been a man's mistress, sold him the house she was living in and they subsequently fell out, it was held that he could compel her to leave.[36]

2. *Joint ownership*

If property is bought in the joint names of cohabitees and the deeds or documents prepared at the time of purchase define the shares which each of them shall have in that property, their ultimate rights in the property are those defined in the deeds. If married people enter into an agreement defining who shall have what, the courts can override such agreement afterwards. But if unmarried people do it, the agreement usually decides the issue, and prudent unmarried people will enter into such agreements before they start. They will, however, be wise to make sure that each is also advised about it by independent solicitors, for a court can upset any agreement if satisfied that one party entered into it as the result of fraud or undue influence by the other.

In many cases of joint ownership the documents merely say (as they do with married people) that the cohabitees are joint owners as tenants in common or as joint tenants. These technical words can hide a series of traps. The first arise while the parties are still alive. *Tenants in common*, without words defining precise shares, implies equal ownership. But if tenants in common have contributed to the purchase of property in cash or its value in unequal shares, a court may still order that they share it in the proportions in which they have contributed.

On the other hand, although *joint tenants*, who own in undivided shares, can acquire a separate interest as tenants in common by serving notice (a notice of severance) on the other joint tenants, the end result by law is a tenancy in common *in equal shares*. The courts cannot go behind that tenancy in common and carve the property up differently to reflect actual contributions.

The second layer of problems may surface when a joint owner dies. If property is held by people as tenants in common the proportionate share of any of them who die passes into their estate. Except in the case of married couples, joint owners can always force a sale of jointly owned property to cash in their interest. But particularly where cohabitees are involved beneficiaries of their estates are often far keener to do that, and far less sympathetic to any surviving cohabitee. If, however, property is still in joint ownership by joint tenants when one of them dies, the whole share of the deceased passes automatically to the survivor or survivors. In either of those cases the only saving grace, for surviving tenants in common and for the beneficiaries of deceased joint tenants, is if they have a right to claim financial provision under the 1975 Inheritance Act (see Chapter 9).

The following cases illustrate the position:

1. Cohabitees bought a property as tenants in common with a 100 per cent mortgage. Each contributed to the acquisition expenses, they sublet most of the house to tenants, and each contributed out of earnings to the running expenses. When they fell out each was entitled to half on the basis of equal contribution.[37]
2. Cohabitees bought in joint names as tenants in common without any defined shares. The woman contributed approximately one-quarter and the man three-quarters of the cost. Their rights in the property were declared to be in those proportions.[38]
3. Cohabitees bought in joint names, and the deed contained provisions commonly used in joint purchase deeds that they owned it beneficially on trust for themselves as joint tenants. The woman, as any joint tenant may do, served notice on her partner terminating the joint tenancy. As we have seen, the effect of such notices is to change ownership into tenancy in common *in equal shares*. The court decided that as there was an express trust in equal shares, the property was to be divided equally and there was no legal basis for enquiry into the proportion in which the two had contributed.[39]
4. A cohabiting couple bought a farm for £40,000 as joint tenants, the woman providing virtually all the money. She later died and her mother attempted to claim her share. The court decided that the whole property had passed to the man on her death as a result of the joint tenancy rules.[40]
5. The rights of a cohabitee who is a joint owner are not confined to sharing the property. A cohabitee who was a joint owner was thrown out of the property by her partner. The court decided that, apart from her share in the property, she could also claim what amounted to a rent to cover the period during which she was deprived of the use of the property.[41]

3. *Implied joint ownership*

Implied joint ownership is the closest which the law goes towards giving cohabitees 'fair shares' in the property acquired during cohabitation. The basic principle is that a cohabitee who can prove that he or she has made a contribution in money or money's-worth to the acquisition of property in the name of his or her partner is entitled to a share in it. But the courts do not have any general power to do what they think is fair and reasonable in the circumstances. So, for example, housekeeping duties and bringing up children were not enough to give a woman, who had lived with a man in a house owned by him for 19 years, any share in the house.[42]

Again, the circumstances where shares have been allowed are best illustrated by decided cases:

1. A married man and the woman he was living with decided to buy land and build a bungalow on it. He bought the land and they both worked together on the house. She demolished a building on the site with a sledgehammer, removed the rubble, worked the cement mixer and painted the house. They were both working and both contributed for a while to mortgage repayments. Then they fell out. The court decided that she was entitled to a third of the value of the house.[43]

2. A woman and a man lived together in the man's house for seven years during which time she contributed to their joint living expenses. The court awarded her a one-fifth share in the house.[44]

3. A woman and a man lived together in a house bought in his name with a 100 per cent mortgage. She wanted the house to be put in joint names but they were both involved in divorce proceedings and he gave that as a reason for having it in his name only. She contributed substantially to the housekeeping costs out of her own earnings, thus making it easier for the man to make the mortgage repayments. When they fell out the court awarded her a half share in the house.[45]

Finally, there is an example which does not involve cohabitees in the general sense. A man bought property in his own name for the joint use of himself, his aunt and her daughter. The aunt and her daughter paid £500 and £250 towards the purchase price and after that contributed weekly to the mortgage repayments and other outgoings. For his part the man carried out a great deal of work to maintain and improve the house. The daughter died and the aunt claimed shares for herself and for the daughter's estate. The court decided that the aunt and daughter's estate should have 30 per cent and 10 per cent respectively and that the man should have 60 per cent.[46]

It will be appreciated from these cases that with implied joint ownership – and with actual joint ownership where no specific shares are declared in trust documents – everything may depend upon the extent to which a cohabitee can prove the value and extent of his or her financial contribution to property as a proportion of its overall cost. General housework is not a contribution to property; but providing money to pay general household bills may be, particularly if that eases the problems of the other cohabitee in paying a mortgage or other property outgoings. And physical contributions to the construction, improvement and maintenance of property will be regarded as contributions having the value of money.

4. Donatio Mortis Causa. A person who hands property over to someone else without clear documentary evidence that a gift is intended usually retains the right to reclaim it (see page 122). But if someone hands property over when at point of death and clearly intends a gift, the recipient acquires the legal right to it. Thus a woman was held entitled to keep the house she shared as cohabitee with her partner after he had given her the deeds on his death bed.[47]

Notes

1. *Wallis* v *Wallis* (1993) *The Times* 5 August
2. See Appendix 1: Section 25(1) Matrimonial Causes Act 1973
3. *K* v *K* (1992) *The Times* 21 February; in Re *F* (minors) (1993) *The Times* 1 December
4. In Re *J* (a minor – property transfer) (1992) *The Times* 12 November
5. See Appendix 2
6. *P* v *P* (1978) All ER 70
7. *Calder* v *Calder* (1976) *The Times* 29 June; see also *Browne* v *Browne* (1988) *The Times* 25 November (husband benefited from wife's trust interests)
8. *Michael* v *Michael* (1986) *The Times* 28 May
9. *Kowalczyk* v *Kowalczyk* (1973) *The Times* 14 April
10. *Parker* v *Parker* (1977) *The Times* 12 March
11. *Martin* v *Martin* (1976) *The Times* 26 February
12. *Wachtel* v *Wachtel* (1973) *The Times* 9 February
13. *Preston* v *Preston* (1981) *The Times* 25 June
14. *S* v *S* (1983) *The Times* 10 May
15. See note 9 above
16. See note 10 above
17. See note 2 above
18. *Greenham* v *Greenham* (1988) *The Times* 22 April
19. *Mesher* v *Mesher* (1973) *The Times* 13 February; *Martin* v *Martin* (1978) Fam 12
20. *Clutton* v *Clutton* (1990) *The Times* 13 November
21. *Walker* v *Hall* (1983) *The Times* 18 July
22. *Harnett* v *Harnett* (1974) 1 All ER 1; *Martin* v *Martin* (1977) 3 All ER 762; and *Mesher* v *Mesher* (1973) *The Times* 13 February
23. *Martin* v *Martin* (1976) 3 All ER 625

24. *Mitchell* v *Mitchell* (1983) *The Times* 6 December
25. *H* v *H* (1974) *The Times* 19 June
26. See note 6 above
27. See note 6 above
28. *Kyte* v *Kyte* (1987) *The Times* 17 August
29. See Appendix 1: Section 25 Matrimonial Causes Act 1973
30. See note 2 above
31. Domestic Violence & Matrimonial Proceedings Act 1976
32. *Davis* v *Johnson* (1978) *The Times* 10 March
33. *Ainsbury* v *Millington* (1985) *The Times* 12 August
34. *Sen* v *Hedley* (1991) *The Times* 6 March
35. *Crane* v *Davis & Anor* (1981) *The Times* 13 May
36. *Chandler* v *Kersely* (1978) *The Times* 14 March
37. *Bernard* v *Josephs* (1982) *The Times* 31 March
38. *Walker* v *Hall* (1983) *The Times* 18 July
39. *Goodman* v *Gallent* (1985) *The Times* 7 November
40. *Barton* v *Morris* (1985) *The Times* 1 May
41. *Dennis* v *MacDonald* (1981) *The Times* 26 February
42. *Burns* v *Burns* (1983) *The Times* 2 August
43. *Cooke* v *Head* (1972) *The Times* 20 January
44. *Hall* v *Hall* (1981) *The Times* 4 April
45. *Grant* v *Edwards* (1986) *The Times* 28 March
46. *Passee* v *Passee* (1987) *The Times* 8 August
47. See note 34 above

Chapter 8

The Clean Break: Court Property Orders and Why They May Pay

Introduction

A clean break occurs when the court makes an order after decree nisi, by consent or of its own decision, that there be no ongoing payment of maintenance between the spouses. Such orders may take effect immediately or after maintenance has been paid for a fixed period – but in the latter case it is essential that the order specifically excludes the right to extend the period.[1] Typically, these orders also exclude the right of either spouse to claim against the estate of the first to die under the Inheritance (Provision for Family & Dependants) Act 1975 (see Chapter 9).

There cannot, however, be any final settlement of children's rights to maintenance or Child Support. Those continue at least until the children reach the age of 17 and may continue after that until their full-time education has finished.

A clean break between the spouses is always desirable. Their marriage has ended. Both are likely to make better lives afterwards if there is no continuing link between them. If spouses want to agree a clean break, there is usually nothing to stop them. But circumstances may make it impossible if one spouse has virtually all the earning power, the other has very little, and they have limited property to compensate for the absence of maintenance.

The attractions of a clean break for the *payer* of maintenance are obvious. But maintenance is frequently not all that it appears to be for the recipient. So before we consider the circumstances in which clean breaks may be wise, or may be ordered by a court, we need to take a cold look at snags which continuing maintenance may involve.

The disadvantages of maintenance

Often maintenance is paid regularly and for years without any problem. But it is always a running sore. In many cases it is not paid, or is paid irregularly.

A whole host of future circumstances may affect maintenance. The payer may remarry, his new wife may not like the burden of maintenance, and she may spur him on in efforts to avoid it. Or his income may come crashing down, and the level of maintenance with it. If maintenance fails, the spouse entitled to it cannot go back to the court and rejig a property order. So if, for example, a wife occupies a house under a Mesher or Martin order which requires that it be sold some years later and that her husband then have 40–50 per cent of the proceeds, he will still have his share in the house even if maintenance has dwindled in the meantime for quite legitimate reasons.

Then there are many cases where there is no practical way of enforcing payment. If the payer has no regular job, and no assets of substance, there may be nothing which any enforcement procedure can grasp to cover arrears. He may disappear abroad and, if he does, the cost of enforcing payment will be substantial even if he can be traced and even if he is in a country which, by treaty, will enforce British maintenance orders. If the payer will in the end have a share in the house, it is possible to apply to the court for an order charging the value of arrears of his share. But that will only produce money when the house is sold.

Unpaid maintenance is a debt. The same procedures, with their strengths and multitude of weaknesses, are available for enforcing its payments as for any other debt. If the payer owns goods which can be seized and sold, the bailiffs can be sent in to take them. If he has a steady job which yields more than he needs for his own subsistence, a court can make an attachment of earnings order under which his employer must deduct the amount stated in the order and pay it to the court. If he has money in a bank, or other money is known to be owed to him, an order (*a garnishee order*) can be obtained compelling the bank or creditor to pay the money direct to the person owed maintenance; the payer's assets may be seized under sequestration procedures. Finally, he may be made bankrupt for non-payment and the threat or actuality of bankruptcy may produce money when all else fails.

But taking any of these steps involves further court procedures and costs – often substantial costs – and if at the end of the day there is nothing for the procedures to act upon, the spouse taking them is landed with the costs as well. Even if an amount is recovered, the legal costs may wipe it out.[2]

The policy of ultimate despair lies in the courts' power to commit a defaulter to prison for non-payment. If a defaulter is committed, that extinguishes the arrears on which he is committed. Many defaulters prefer prison and our prison population includes several thousand of them.

If spouses entitled to maintenance are reduced to destitution by non-payment, they may apply to the DSS for Income or Family Support. But in that case the DSS is entitled to receive the maintenance to offset the cost – as or when it can be recovered – and there may be delays, and part of social security support may be withheld while things are sorted out. If the payer of maintenance pays erratically, the DSS may only be able to keep up with the overall position in arrears, and the maintained spouse may have to manage with an equally erratic income. As or when arrears are recovered they will go to the DSS first if they relate to periods when social security support has been paid. Only fairly recently have the courts decided that the DSS may claim arrears which arose before the spouse claimed social security benefit, but which were actually paid while the spouse was receiving such benefit.[3]

The advantages of clean break and property orders

Court orders generally

A court order finalising your property position, clean break or not, is an important general protection. No property transaction is final and binding between the two of you unless it is ordered or approved by the court after decree nisi in divorce or nullity, or decree in the case of a formal High Court decree of judicial separation. So until such an order is made the court can rearrange things, even if done by prior agreement. However, if prior arrangements are obviously sensible, and particularly if neither you nor your partner challenges them, the court will usually approve prior deals by formal order.

A court order will also make a radical difference to your rights and liabilities against third parties. If you transfer property to your partner voluntarily, that may in law be regarded as a gift. If, on the other hand, it is transferred to your partner under a court order, even if agreed, it will be a transfer for valuable consideration – in settlement of the respective property claims – and will not be a gift. Liabilities to Capital Gains Tax, Stamp Duty and inheritance tax may differ, depending on whether or not a gift is involved.

But, more important, if your partner should subsequently become bankrupt, his or her creditors, through the trustee in bankruptcy, may be able to reach back and reclaim certain gifts for the benefit of the creditors. If the property has been transferred under a court order, that is not possible. So, for example, in a case where a court order had been made by consent on previously agreed terms, a husband became bankrupt and his trustee in bankruptcy tried to reclaim part of the property transferred to the wife. The court decided that the order under which it was transferred protected her against this claim.[4] If the property had merely been transferred to her without an approving court order, the trustee in bankruptcy would have had a claim to it under bankruptcy rules.

Clean break orders

Where family assets are significant, it is likely to be possible to put a price on the value of a clean break – related to the maintenance which would otherwise be payable – which compensates in whole or in part for abandoning maintenance. Quite simply, the spouse who might otherwise receive maintenance has a larger slice of the property available than he or she would have if maintenance remained a live issue. A bird in the hand is undoubtedly worth two in the bush between estranged spouses and former spouses particularly because of the problems which may later crop up with maintenance.

But even where little or no compensation is available, clean break orders may still avoid some of the problems already outlined if either of you later have to apply to the DSS for Income or Family Support. If you have reached a final settlement with your former spouse which has been approved by the court there is no ongoing liability on either of you to maintain the other; neither of you is a liable relative if the other has to claim social security benefits. If your partner later has to claim Income Support or Family Support the DSS may not then exercise its separate rights against you to recover all or part of the cost from you as a liable relative, though it may, of course, still recover Child Support. It is important for both of you to remember this, and not merely the one who, at the time of divorce, might otherwise expect maintenance. Wives as well as husbands may be liable for maintenance and positions can reverse.

In addition, clean break orders may eliminate the risk of future claims by your former spouse against your estate under the Inheritance (Provision for Family & Dependants) Act 1975 as long as they specifically say that those rights are included in the settlement.

Finally, your future relations with your partner may be less traumatic if maintenance is no longer payable between you. That may be particularly important if you have children.

It is against this background that you must consider whether a clean break is sensible, even if you do not particularly want one, and even if, on paper, you might be better off with maintenance.

Cash compensation for maintenance on clean break deals or orders

It is possible to determine what maintenance would be payable and then assess a capital value for it. When resources exist which allow a compensatory deal this may form part of a clean break exercise if one is being negotiated or a court is considering whether to order one.

One way of approaching this is to consider what it would cost to buy an annuity which would pay the amount of maintenance, and use that capital figure as a basis for balancing up capital shares. But an annuity pays income for life, and unless the spouses are well on in years, calculating on the basis of a lifetime's maintenance is likely to result in excessive figures.

If a woman's husband is killed in a fatal accident caused by someone else's negligence, for example, the most she is likely to be able to claim against the negligent person is the value of her husband's support (ie his net income less that part which would have been spent to support him) for about 14 years. And that figure is then discounted to allow for the fact that it is paid in advance.

In practice, maintenance orders only run on average for about eight years anyway – spouses remarry, spouses paying maintenance fall on hard times, or spouses receiving maintenance establish themselves financially, so that maintenance of any substance ceases to be relevant. So a maximum of eight years may well be appropriate in any case where the spouse who might otherwise receive maintenance is not yet past her or his mid-40s. Even shorter periods of 'compensation' may be appropriate. In Scotland the basic rule now is that maintenance should be paid for a maximum of three years and that period is increasingly common in English cases.[5]

It may, of course, be that when the capital value of maintenance is calculated, there is not enough cash and property, over and above what the spouse entitled to maintenance might have received anyway, to compensate him or her adequately for forgoing maintenance. But a clean break may still be sensible. And this may particularly be the case for those with children in their care, for whom maintenance will anyway be payable until they finish school, and who will be able to increase their own incomes as the children grow older.

Circumstances which may indicate a clean break

First we look at the sort of circumstances where a negotiated deal may be practical or sensible, and then at those where a court may order a clean break even if one is not agreed.

Agreed clean breaks

1. Where spouses are rich, problems rarely arise. We have already referred several times to the husband who had assets of £2.1 million; he and his wife, both 67, agreed on a clean break. She did not ask for maintenance, and the court ordered that she should have capital of £375,000.[6] At her age she was well able to provide everything which she might reasonably need for the rest of her life with £375,000.
2. Where spouses are both established in separate employments and their respective incomes are such that nominal maintenance is all that would be ordered anyway, a clean break is also usually appropriate. The price of a clean break in such cases is usually an equal split of their property unless it is so substantial as to take them into the arena of the rich, since there is no real case for compensating for maintenance which in any event would not be payable.
3. Even where incomes are such that maintenance might be payable, a clean break is often sensible in exchange for a larger slice of the capital available. For example, a husband may have a larger income, a wife a smaller income and they may not have much property apart from their house. Instead of sharing the value of the house 50:50, for example, with a continuing maintenance obligation, it may make sense all round for the wife to have 70, 80, 90 per cent or indeed the whole house and no maintenance.
4. A clean break may also be sensible, paradoxically, for spouses who have very little. There is little point in maintenance if both are already living, and are likely to have to go on living, on DSS Income

or Family Support. And there is no advantage to either of the spouses, and there is the risk of continuing hassle, if the one entitled to maintenance will in any event still depend on Income Support, and the one paying it has a low income which will only justify a small order. If maintenance is paid, it will only reduce the recipient's means tested benefits with no practical advantage to the recipient. And the fact that it is payable may mean that the recipient has to do without until the DSS accept the fact and make up benefit accordingly.

Inevitably, the default rate is very high indeed when payers themselves have low incomes and live all the time under financial pressures which make the payment of maintenance an obvious and extremely painful additional burden. Spouses entitled to maintenance in these circumstances may do themselves a good turn by agreeing a clean break even if the contents of the home or something like that is all they get out of it. At least the right to maintenance will not then complicate their straightforward right to Income Support – or Family Support if they are working but earning a low wage.

Compulsory clean breaks

The courts' powers to order a clean break under the law are described in Chapter 4. But in many cases where it would be sensible for the parties to agree a clean break a court will not compel one if either of them resists the application. A court may be impressed by the argument that maintenance will not make any practical difference to the parties because either or both of them will have to depend on Income or Family Support anyway.[7] But another may take the view that maintenance should still be ordered because it will reduce the burden on the state.

The courts could, of course, be equally variable when considering agreed clean break orders. They still have to receive full details of the parties' means. But if a clean break order is agreed, almost invariably it will be made.

The reason for the difference lies in the basic policy which resulted in the courts' power to make clean break orders:

> 'Parliament must be presumed to have intended that the court should be allowed maximum freedom to help former spouses to pursue independent lives liberated from the running irritant of financial interdependence.'[8]

If the parties show any sign of harmony by agreeing anything, the courts will be reluctant to refuse to implement it.

It is unfortunate but true that, when it comes to the crunch of making clean break orders when the parties have *not* agreed, the courts have proved reluctant to intervene where resources do not allow a capital deal to compensate for the absence of maintenance. Thus we have the 1988 case previously referred to in which the court refused a clean break in a case where the wife was established as a teacher earning more than £10,000 a year, and the husband's circumstances had been so reduced following redundancy that he was only paying a nominal 5p a year maintenance anyway.[9] Admittedly that was an extreme (and probably wrong), decision. It would sound the death knell for clean break decisions in virtually all cases if judges felt entitled to take the view that 'maintenance orders should be kept alive in case unforeseen contingencies deprived a wife of the ability to provide for herself'.

Nevertheless, at present that mostly seems to be the case. Usually, the courts will only order a clean break against the wishes of a spouse who will lose a right to maintenance if cash or property is offered in sufficient value to compensate for its loss or – sometimes – if there is nothing there at all. As a result, compulsory clean break orders at present seem to be limited to cases where the spouse liable to maintenance is relatively rich or is broke. On the other hand, it has to be remembered that because clean breaks are agreed in the vast majority of cases where they are sensible, only a handful of cases are decided by the courts and are reported. Almost by definition these cases will be the difficult ones.

If a substantial sum is available, a clean break may be ordered even if there are still dependent children.[10] And the fact that Section 25 says that first consideration must be given to the interests of children does not in any case override the objective of obtaining a clean break between the parents. However, where there are dependent children there is always an element of unreality in clean break orders. Child Support and the children's right to maintenance continues and cannot be compromised.

In considering any contested clean break application, the courts will, however, concentrate specifically on the words of Section 25A – whether the spouse losing maintenance can 'adjust without undue hardship to the termination of his or her financial dependence'. Other justifications will not do.

So, for example, the court rejected on appeal a clean break which had been ordered (one suspects in the despair with which such cases are often considered) to 'bring to an end an acrimonious dispute between a former husband and wife'.[11]

Notes

1. *Richardson* v *Richardson* (1994) Family Law 268
2. *Clark* v *Clark* (1988) *The Times* 31 March
3. *McCorquodale* v *Chief Administrator* (1988) *The Times* 3 May
4. Re *Abbott* (1982) 3 All ER 183
5. See Appendix 2: Section 9(1)(d) Family Law (Scotland) Act 1985
6. *S* v *S* (1983) *The Times* 10 May; see too *Duxbury* v *Duxbury* (1987) 1 FLR
7. *Delaney* v *Delaney* (1990) *The Times* 4 June; *Ashley* v *Blackburn* (1988) *Law Society Gazette* 20 October
8. *S* v *S* (1986) *The Times* 9 July
9. *Whiting* v *Whiting* (1988) *The Times* 29 January
10. *Suter* v *Suter & Jones* (1987) *The Times* 9 January
11. *Morris* v *Morris* (1985) *The Times* 17 June

Chapter 9

Wills and Inheritance

Introduction

None of us expects to die. But sooner or later all of us do and when that happens someone else becomes legally entitled to any property we have. If we are married or living with someone, our partner is likely to figure prominently among those we wish to have or share our estate. But if that relationship breaks down, he or she is not likely to figure at all. Decree absolute in divorce ends any inheritance rights of the surviving spouse under the will or on the intestacy of the other. And remarriage revokes any will made before the remarriage. But before that original rights continue.

Since people do die after relationships break down and before all their property tangles have been resolved – indeed, some cases where this has happened have cropped up in previous chapters – it is important to consider with some urgency who will have what in the event of one's death.

Basic cautions

Some basic cautions serve to emphasise this message:

1. If spouses or cohabitees own property in joint names on terms which will legally pass their interest in property automatically to the survivor if they die (eg the joint tenancy of a house already discussed in connection with cohabitees' property) that interest will continue to pass automatically unless or until notices are served or accounts changed which cancel that effect.
2. A long time may elapse between the collapse of a marriage and decree absolute in divorce. If a spouse has made a will leaving property to his or her partner, or appointing that partner an executor of the will, that partner will be entitled to inherit the property or act as executor until decree absolute in divorce is granted.

3. Inheritance rights are not affected if cohabitees part. So if a cohabitee has made a will leaving property to his or her partner, or appointing him or her executor, that cohabitee will continue to be entitled to the property, or to act as executor, until the will is revoked – for example, by destroying it with that intention, or making a new will.

4. If a spouse has not made a will, his or her partner will continue to be entitled to the substantial inheritance rights of a spouse which arise under the Intestacy Acts until decree absolute. Until then, he or she will also continue to have the first right to act as administrator of the deceased spouse's estate – the equivalent of being an executor when there is no will.

5. A cohabitee, however, has no right to inherit on intestacy or to be an administrator of the estate unless that cohabitee was also in a blood relationship with his or her former partner which ranks for an inheritance under the Intestacy Act.

6. Whether or not there is a will, certain people can apply to the court for reasonable financial provision out of the estate of a deceased person. These rights arise under the Inheritance (Provision for Family & Dependants) Act 1975. If established, they have priority over gifts made by wills or arising under the laws of intestacy. But the Act creates a *right to claim* not a right to inherit. The people who can claim are the following:

    (a) unless the parties have been separated by a High Court decree of judicial separation, a surviving spouse may claim such provision as is reasonable in all the circumstances if such provision is not made by will, or does not result under the laws of intestacy

    (b) the following may also claim but only if a will or the laws of intestacy fail reasonable provision for their *maintenance*:
    - a spouse separated under High Court decree of judicial separation
    - a divorced former spouse who has not remarried unless a clean break order excludes the right
    - a child of the deceased (now also including a child born out of wedlock)
    - a person who at any time was treated by the deceased as his or her child in his or her marriage
    - any other person who was being maintained in whole or in part by the deceased immediately before death. This category includes cohabitees living with the deceased at the date of death and frequently sets the scene for conflict between cohabitees, spouses or former spouses, and

children who might otherwise inherit under a will or the rules of intestacy, or who themselves have claims under the 1975 Act.

7. One particular legal rule can turn inheritance into a complete lottery. It applies whether there is a will or not, though if a properly drawn will starts off with a gift to a spouse or cohabiting partner, it is usual to cover the problem by making the gift conditional on that spouse or partner surviving for 28 days. The rule is that if two people die in an accident – road accidents and fires at home are common examples – and it is impossible to decide who died first, the younger is presumed to survive the older. So if a couple are killed and the man is older, his property may pass to the woman if his will gives it, or, if they are married, under a will or the rules of intestacy. And it will then pass with her property to whoever is entitled to her estate.

It is particularly important for people already in second and subsequent marriages or relationships to remember these cautions. Suppose, for example, a man has children by an earlier marriage. If he dies first, or is presumed to die first, and he has no will which takes care of the problem, his property will pass to his wife and will then pass on as her will directs, or to *her* blood relatives if she has no will. His children and any new partner may be out in the cold. Equally, if people in unmarried relationships do not make wills, the survivor has no absolute right to claim as a spouse or, usually, as a blood relative.

Very soon we shall look specifically at the mechanics of wills, intestacy and the Inheritance (Provision for Family & Dependants) Act 1975, but first it is important to emphasise the steps you should consider taking as soon as any relationship breaks down:

1. Whether or not you are married, review everything which you have in joint names: property, building society or bank accounts and anything else. Give instructions to any bank, building society or similar account-holder not to make any payments out of any joint account in the future without your signature. Give notices ending any other joint ownership, and if you are not absolutely sure how to do that, ask for a solicitor's help.
2. Make a will, or a new will. You can make a will yourself, and we shall come to that, but in this particular instance it is wise to have a solicitor's advice. You may have to design your will to protect your estate as far as possible from claims under the 1975 Act – and, even more important, the substantial costs against your estate which may arise if such claims are made. A statement

accompanying your will which explains in detail why you have made it the way you have may be an important protection for those you do want to benefit.

Many people attempt a more obvious solution by giving their property to those they want to have it before they die. But that offers no guaranteed answer, for if the gift was made within ten years of the date of death and a court decides that it was made to defeat someone else's right to claim under the 1975 Act, the court can reach back and reverse the gift. We return to the detailed effects of the 1975 Act later. The court can also order that property which has passed to a surviving joint tenant by survivorship (see Chapter 7, pages 123–6) shall nevertheless be treated as part of the estate of the deceased.[1]

Now let us look in detail at the mechanics of the things which figure in the cautions and warnings already given.

Specifics

Wills

It is not essential to have a solicitor to draw up your will, but wills have to be made with meticulous attention to detail laid down by law if they are to be valid. And even if they are valid, the way things are said may result in totally unexpected legal or tax complications. Sorting these out may cost your estate a small fortune compared with the cost of having your will made by a solicitor. So unless you are sure of your ground it is sensible to ask a solicitor to make your will – he, after all, has been professionally trained to deal with the task. And even if you are sure, keep it simple and straightforward. The more complicated you try to make things, the more likely you are to leave unpleasant surprises for those you wish to benefit.

As to solicitors, charges for making wills vary widely and there is no fixed rate. On the other hand, any solicitor ought to quote a price for making a will, and you should not be afraid to ask, or to shop around, if you wish.

If you wish to do it yourself, you can buy a printed blank will from law stationers and from many other stationers. These forms usually include all the basic instructions and if you follow these meticulously – and still keep it simple – you should end up with a valid will.

But you can start with a blank sheet of paper. Your will must be in writing and if possible should be written out without any alterations.

If any are made, they should be initialled by you and by the two people who witness the will when it is signed. If there is any question of the will having been altered after it is signed, it may make it invalid altogether; or the alteration may be ignored and what was written originally may take effect.

It is sensible to follow the sequence conventional in wills so we will describe that sequence, using fictitious names and addresses.

A will usually starts with the full name of the person making it:

'This will is made by me JANE MARY JONES of 44 Tudor Gardens, Ripon in the County of York.'

Next it is usual to make it clear that no other earlier will or codicil (which is a change to a will which must be made in exactly the same way as a will) shall have effect:

1. I revoke all former wills and testamentary dispositions.

Next it is usual to appoint an *executor* or executors. Any person over 18 who is solvent and of sound mind may be an executor, including a person who is a beneficiary. Where everything is given to one person it is common to make that person executor as well. But if the property is to go to children under 18, people usually pick members of their family or close and trusted friends. A will can take effect even if executors are not named, but not naming them adds to cost and trouble. The executors are the people who have the legal right to obtain probate of the will which gives it official sanction.

The right of executors to deal with the estate derives from the will itself. So, from the moment the person who has made the will dies, they, unlike administrators of a person who has died without a will, can start sorting out the deceased's affairs. They can, for example, give instructions to change the insurance on a car, which may be very important if only the deceased was insured and other members of the family now need to drive it. But there are many things which executors cannot do without obtaining and being able to produce *probate* of the will which establishes that it has been formally 'proved' to the Probate Court. For example, they cannot sell any house or land which the deceased owned and they cannot *demand* that money which he or she held in deposit or other accounts be paid to them.

So if executors cannot collect in, or deal with, all the deceased's property without probate, they have to obtain it. This is not the place for a detailed discussion of the processes of probate. If executors instruct a solicitor to obtain probate for them, he will deal with all the technicalities. If they decide to do it themselves, the personal applications department of their local Probate Registry – whose address appears in the telephone directory under 'Probate Registry' – will tell them what they have to do.

Armed with the authority of probate, executors have a complete legal right to collect in all the deceased's assets, and the duty to pay out of them all his or her debts, and distribute the balance to the people named as beneficiaries in the will. If the debts are greater than the value of the estate, the estate has to be sorted out as an insolvent estate. No one else is legally liable for the debts of the deceased, but if an estate is insolvent, executors may be wise to leave the problems to the creditors, not touch the estate, and not apply for probate themselves. If they intermeddle with the estate, the creditors can require them to account for all they have done and for any asset they have received.

The will continues with the appointment of executors:

2. I appoint my brother John James of 34 Spring Gardens in the City of Warwick and my sister Mary Smith of 21 New Terrace in the City of Bath to be my executors.

Then the will spells out who is to have the estate. This is where it is particularly important if you are making your own will to use simple and straightforward words. For example:

'I give everything I have to my two children Peter Martin Jones and June Mary Jones in equal shares.'

Next it is usual to put in a clause which includes the date when the will is signed. Here a bit of legalese may be forgiven:

'In witness whereof I have hereunto set my hand this   day of   One Thousand Nine Hundred and

Finally, the signature. Here there are several absolute essentials:

(a) A will must not be witnessed by a person who is named as a beneficiary in the will, or by the husband or wife of such a person. If it is, they lose the benefit under the will.
(b) The date when the will is being signed should be written into the date clause already described.
(c) The person making the will *must* sign it at the end of the text (ie not leaving any space where anything else might be written in) in the presence of two witnesses over 18.
(d) The two witnesses must then also sign it.
(e) All three of them must remain present until all three have signed, so that each also witnesses the signatures of the other two. If one witness signs and then nips off to do something else before the other two have signed, the will is not valid.

(f) The witnesses should write their addresses and occupations below their signatures.

If the will is signed like this, it will be valid. But it will then be necessary for proper signature to be formally proved before probate can be obtained. So it is universal practice to include words at the end of the will to save the need for formal proof. These words are usually written on one side of the paper immediately after the text of the will ends so that the person signing the will can sign alongside them and the witnesses can sign below them. So Jane Jones's will would have, below the date clause:

'SIGNED by JANE
MARY JONES in our
presence and attested
by us in the presence
of her and each other'

When everything is dated and signed the will is complete.

The will is now an important document. It should be kept safe. If Jane Jones's house catches fire and she dies in the fire, her prudence in making a will will be lost if it also goes up in smoke. So it is sensible to leave the will with a bank, solicitor or other person with facilities for keeping it safe. And it is also sensible to make sure that other people, particularly the executors, know that it exists, know where it is and have exact copies of it which include copies of all signatures and details of the witnesses. If the original should then be lost, probate may be obtained on a copy.

Intestate succession

Inheritance when there is no will, or none can be found or is known to exist

If you do not make a will, the right to your property passes to any relatives you have in order of preference defined by the Intestates Estate Act. If you have no relatives in the long list of alternatives, it passes to the Crown. Surviving spouses have first claim, but if you have no surviving spouse, your property goes to *your* blood relatives. Blood relatives of your spouse do not enter into the picture.

If there is no will, no one has the legal right to deal with your estate until they have been appointed *administrator* of your estate under *letters of administration* obtained, as with a probate, from the Probate

Registry. Unlike executors, whose basic title derives from the will naming them, potential administrators cannot start dealing with your estate before then. The right to apply for letters of administration lies with those ranking in the first line for inheritance under the rules of intestacy.

The rules of inheritance on intestacy are therefore very important and we will look at them now.

(a) If you have a surviving spouse

Who has the right to what depends on who survives.

(a) If you have a surviving spouse, no children, no issue of children, no surviving parent, no brothers and sisters of the whole blood (ie you have both parents in common), and no issue of them – nieces and nephews – your spouse will be entitled to everything you leave.

(b) If you have a surviving spouse, no children or issue of children, but you have relatives in the other categories, your spouse will be entitled to your personal property in the house and the first £200,000 of your estate. If there is more, he or she will also be entitled to the investment income of half the capital of the remainder for life. The rest – the other half immediately, and the remainder following the surviving spouse's death – will go to your parents if they survive you. Otherwise it will go to your brothers and sisters or their issue.

(c) If you have children, your surviving spouse will be entitled to your personal property in the house and the first £125,000 of your estate. Again, he or she will be entitled to investment income generated by half of anything above that for life. Your children will take the other half immediately, and the capital which pays the life income when your spouse dies.

The specific figures – £200,000 and £125,000 – are increased from time to time to allow for inflation. The last increase (applying only to deaths after the increase) was on 1 December 1993. House values alone may still mean that in many cases the rules of intestacy will not ensure that your surviving spouse becomes complete owner even of the house if previously it was only in your name. If that is so, he or she may be driven to make a costly application to the court under the Inheritance (Provision for Family & Dependants) Act 1975 (to which we come shortly) to secure his or her own position. A will can save that problem.

(b) If you have no surviving spouse

With spouses out of the way, the problem becomes a little simpler:

(a) If you are survived by your children or your children's children, they take all your property, children's children taking the share their parent would have had and so on.

(b) If you have no one in the children's category but your parents survive you, everything goes to them – equally if both survive, so if they are divorced you may have something to think about.

(c) If you have no one in the children's or parents' category, everything goes to your surviving brothers and sisters of the whole blood and to the children of any who die before you do. Again, their children take the share their parent would have had.

(d) If you have no one in the previous categories but have brothers or sisters of the half blood (ie you have one parent in common with them) they or their children take everything.

(e) If you have no one in the previous categories but are survived by grandparents, they take everything.

(f) If you have no one in the previous categories but are survived by uncles or aunts of the whole blood (ie brothers or sisters of either of your parents) or their issue, they take everything.

(g) if you have no one in the previous categories but are survived by uncles or aunts of the half blood (ie half brothers or sisters of either of your parents) or their issue, they take everything.

If there is no one in any of these categories, your property goes to the Crown, although the Crown may sometimes by concession (granted, if at all, on application) allow all or part of it to someone close to you who satisfies the Crown that the circumstances are such that provision is reasonable.

You will see, therefore, that the law holds out a fairly wide net to catch the estates of people who do not make wills. But who gets what may be very arbitrary, and a large part of your estate may be spent in the cost of tracing people and proving whether or not they survived you when more distant relatives come into the picture. Moreover, if a relative who qualifies to inherit is known to exist or to have existed, but he or she cannot be found, his share in your estate may be frozen unless or until he can be found. Very substantial sums of money are deposited in the Chancery Division of the High Court for such people – hence the phrase 'money in chancery'.

A properly made will may save your family these problems.

The Inheritance (Provision for Family & Dependants) Act 1975

We have so far considered the position of people who have the *right* to inherit your estate either because you have named them as beneficiaries under your will, or under the rules of intestacy if you have not made a will. We now turn to those who may have the right *to claim* provision out of your estate – the people we have already listed in the basic cautions at the beginning of this chapter. By the time the 1975 Act becomes relevant to your affairs, you will have lost any tangible interest in what is happening, but your family will not, so the mechanics of the 1975 Act are important for them.

1. *Another basic caution*

Here again there is an important basic caution for you if you are a survivor possibly entitled to claim – spouse, former spouse, cohabitee, child and so on. If a claim on an estate is not made by starting court proceedings within six months of the date when probate or letters of administration are granted, the right to claim may be lost.[2] The court has the power to allow a claim outside that period and will normally allow it if the estate will lose nothing but the value of the time-limit and the person applying will otherwise suffer great hardship. But the longer things are left, the less likely it is that the time-limit will be waived; indeed, the estate may well have been distributed making that difficult or impossible.

Legal aid is available for such proceedings for people whose means are limited and these claims are not claims which anyone who is not legally trained is likely to be able to handle on their own. So the rule must be to see a solicitor immediately someone dies if you may have a right to claim on their estate. Your claim may well be settled by negotiation before it has to go anywhere near a court – many are – but unless your court application is made in time you may lose any basis even to negotiate.

2. *What can a court order?*

A court can make the same sort of orders as it can in divorce:[3] maintenance, lump sum payment, property transfer and settlement of property. It can also vary a marriage settlement. So if attempts are made to negotiate an agreed solution to a claim, all or any of these may be part of the negotiation.

3. *How are claims decided?*

First of all, surviving spouses have the edge on other possible claimants because, as already noted, they can claim 'reasonable provision' while other claimants can only claim 'reasonable provision for their maintenance'. But maintenance in this context does not mean that the provision has to be by periodic instalments. The courts can and do order lump sum payments and property transfers in favour of people who only qualify for maintenance.

The basis which the law lays down for its decisions has a very similar quality to the basis for decisions in divorce. The court has to have regard to a number of things and there are no hard-and-fast rules or guidelines. Indeed, between spouses the court is specifically required to consider what the survivor might have been entitled to had the marriage been ended by divorce rather than death.[4]

In all cases the court is also concerned with a balancing act – the interest of the claimant or claimants against the interest of those who would otherwise benefit from the estate if it passed as directed by any will or by the rules of intestacy. So the whole existing financial position of the claimant and of the beneficiaries comes into the picture.

The matters to which the court is required to have regard are essentially these:[5]

(a) the financial resources and needs of the person or persons applying
(b) those of any beneficiary under a will or the rules of intestacy
(c) the deceased's obligations to any person claiming and to any beneficiaries of the estate and any disability from which any of them suffer
(d) the size and nature of the estate
(e) anything else, including the conduct of anyone involved, which the court considers relevant.

The way people have behaved may enter into it so if you are making a will which excludes or gives short shift to someone who might have a claim on your estate, a solicitor may advise you to include with the will a statement setting out in detail why you have made your will in the terms which you have. Such statements are often a sensible precaution. They may later help those you do want to benefit stave off claims by those you do not.

Where claims are made by spouses or divorced former spouses the court must also consider:[6]

(a) the duration of the marriage and the age of the spouse who is claiming, and
(b) the contributions which the spouses made to the marriage and, as already noted, what the claimant might have received if divorce and not death had ended the marriage.

Where children or people brought up as children claim, the court also has to consider:[7]

(a) their educational expectations
(b) the extent and length of time of any maintenance of the claimant by the deceased
(c) if a non-blood child is involved, whether the deceased knew it was not his child
(d) if anyone else has a liability to maintain the person applying.

But children's rights are not limited to children under 18 or still in full-time education. Adult children can and do claim, particularly in cases where they might otherwise lose out because their deceased parent has acquired a new partner.

With any other claimant – and this applies particularly to surviving cohabitees and to divorced spouses who did not have a clean break and have not remarried – the court must also consider the basis and extent of the deceased's support for them and the length of time it continued.

4. *The menace of costs and examples from cases*

The total costs of claims under the 1975 Act – and frequently of all parties involved – usually come out of the estate. These costs can escalate rapidly, particularly if many contesting claimants are involved, each with their separate lawyers; they can soon make a dent even in substantial estates and can wipe out small ones altogether. So there is a very powerful incentive for everyone involved to agree to settle claims quickly and often to agree to pay something at least, even on claims which seem to have little merit. Usually settlements are based on figures advised by counsel (barristers) who specialise in this field. The fact that relatively few cases are brought to court, and most of them are settled, means that few court decisions reach the law reports.

However, the following will give some idea of the problem:

1. A woman had a child by a divorced man when she was 18 and agreed to the child being adopted. He had a child of his own by his former marriage and that child was living with him. The woman then lived with the man for four years looking after the child by his marriage and had another child of her own. Then the man died without making a will and the child of the marriage returned to his mother. The man left property worth between £25,000 and £35,000. The woman was awarded £5,000 and the remainder of the estate was divided equally between the two children.[8]

2. A widower had a daughter by his marriage. When the daughter was already grown up he went to live with another woman and subsequently married her. He made a will leaving his wife all his property, and when he died she inherited it. His second wife never had any children of her own, and although she was friendly with the widower's daughter she had never brought her up or looked after her. The second wife then died without making a will. She left an estate of £45,000. The widower's daughter was then 55 and in good health. She applied for provision out of her stepmother's estate and was awarded £19,000.[9] This case is important because it shows how the courts may apply the Act to ensure that stepchildren are not disinherited by remarriage.

3. A woman went to live with a married man as his mistress. He was a lot older than she was and a lot richer. While they were living together he made several promises to provide for her. But after five years the relationship crumbled and they parted, and when he died two years later his will left her nothing. He left £365,000 but because they were not living together when he died and because he had not provided anything for her during the two previous years she did not come into any of the categories of people entitled to claim under the 1975 Act. She got nothing.[10]

4. A twice-married man had a son by his first marriage who was in poor health and living alone in a small flat on social security benefit. The man had two more sons by his second marriage who were adult and in good health, and was survived by them and his wife when he died. His only property of substance was the house in which he had lived with his second wife and their children. The second wife was then 45. She was working and earning £4,500 a year (this was in 1987). The man made a will leaving his property to his widow and three children in four equal shares. The widow

claimed everything and her two sons supported her claim. The court decided that the will did not provide for her adequately, and that she should at least remain secure in her home. The most which could be raised by a mortgage which she could afford was £7,500. The son by the previous marriage was awarded £7,500, and the widow was awarded the rest.[11]

5. Conclusions on the 1975 Act

The number and variety of conflicting claims which may arise because of the 1975 Act are so large, and the number of reported cases so small, that it is not possible to offer any specific guidelines as to how any particular case may be approached. However, the reported decisions do show that a court is likely to use the Act to make sure that people who, on a common sense basis, should benefit from an estate, do so. Insofar as there is any bias, the law itself creates a bias in favour of surviving spouses. But beyond that the closeness of the relationship is likely to be what matters in deciding the priorities. So cohabitees' rights become stronger the longer they live with their partner; and children, stepchildren and people treated as children are likely to have claims which are stronger than those of more distant relatives or beneficiaries under a will.

What amounts may be awarded?

If the claim is by a surviving spouse and there are no other competing claims under the 1975 Act, that spouse's rights are likely to be decided on the same principles as would have been applied if the marriage had ended in divorce – because the Act specifically says so. The earlier chapters which deal with financial provision in divorce will give some guide as to amounts, although in the case of death ongoing maintenance is unlikely, and capital provision may be correspondingly increased as it is in clean break settlements.

Where other claims arise the position is likely to be far more complicated, particularly where claimants of comparable rank – surviving spouses, long-established surviving cohabitees, and former spouses – are involved. These will inevitably be decided with an eye to the value of the estate, but the proportions awarded, in these more than most family law cases, will usually depend ultimately on the gut reaction of the individual making the decision. Of course, lawyers have gut reactions which are 'educated' to such tasks. And since few of these cases go as far as to test the gut reactions of judges, they are mostly settled on the advice given, sometimes by the solicitors involved, but more frequently by experienced barristers from whom those solicitors seek advice on behalf of their clients. Usually, the cost of not taking that advice is so high that the clients take it and agree to settle on the advice they have received. Frankly, there is usually little else that they can sensibly do.

Notes

1. Sections 9 and 10 Inheritance (Provision for Family & Dependants) Act 1975; see too *Jessop* v *Jessop* (1991) *The Times* 16 October
2. Section 4
3. Section 2
4. Section 3(2); see *Moody* v *Stevenson* (1991) *The Times* 30 July
5. Section 3(1)
6. Sections 3(2) and 3(3)
7. See note 6 above
8. *CA & Anor* v *CC & Others* (1978) *The Times* 18 November
9. In Re *Leach Deceased* (1985) *The Times* 12 April
10. *Layton* v *Martin & Others* (1985) *The Times* 11 December
11. *Rajabally* v *Rajabally* (1987) *The Times* 18 March

Children – Parental Responsibility, Residence, Contact, Maintenance, Adoption, Local Authority Care and Wardship

Introduction

A person remains a child until he or she reaches the age of 18, although the obligation to maintain a child may continue after that date so long as the child is in full-time education.

Since the Family Law Reform Act 1987 came into force[1] the historic distinctions between children born out of marriage and those born within marriage have been virtually eliminated. The only exception is that property which passes with peerages or other titles will still only pass to children born of a marriage on which inheritance depends.[2]

So rights under deeds, wills and other documents made after 3 March 1988 will pass to children or the descendants of children regardless of whether or not their parents were married – so long, of course, as it can be proved who their parents were. Similarly, the right to claim from estates on intestacy, or under the Inheritance (Provision for Family & Dependants) Act 1975, is the same for children and the descendants of children regardless of whether or not their parents were married.

Finally, parents may now use the same procedures in seeking children's orders, whether or not they are or ever were married.[3] Children over 18 who are still in full-time education may themselves, in certain circumstances, claim maintenance against their parents.[4]

The only difference which the status of parents now makes relates to the proof of paternity. Fathers may apply to the court for an order granting them parental responsibility of any child of an unmarried relationship.[5] New procedures have also been created under which fathers may apply to be registered as such on children's birth certificates.[6] And a person may apply to the court for a declaration of parentage where that is in doubt.[7]

Of course, identifying themselves as the father of a child is the last thing which some men want to do, particularly if, as a result, they must then maintain the child. But genetic fingerprinting can now prove conclusively whether a particular individual is the parent of a child or child of a parent. Genetic fingerprinting can be carried out so long as blood or tissue samples are available from the parent and the child. So the courts now have the power, extended to include samples of body fluid or tissue other than blood, to order that such samples be provided in any proceedings where parentage is questioned.[8] Any individual who refuses to comply with such an order is likely to find that the court will then assume that the sample would have proved what he or she otherwise wished to deny.[9]

Where, however, a married woman conceives a child by artificial insemination with the consent of her husband, that child is now to be treated as the child of the woman and her husband.[10] So no man who has consented to his wife using AID should think that he can later gain an advantage by using tests to prove that he is not the father of any child which results.

As a result of the 1987 Act, the question of whether or not the parents of any child were married no longer makes any practical difference to the procedures and principles which will be involved if any question of residence, contact, maintenance or other financial provision for the child arises.

The basic principles

If a court has to consider any question involving the residence or upbringing of a child, or its property or income, the law says that the child's welfare must be the first and paramount consideration.[11] A court is not entitled to consider whether, from any other point of view, the claims of the father may be superior to those of the mother, or the claims of the mother superior to the father.

If asked to decide, the courts will do their best to achieve what the law says. But, unfortunately, the way in which issues involving children have to be brought to court sometimes confuses the parents' view of how these objectives are approached. For children's best interests are often decided in cases brought as a spin-off of divorce or separation proceedings which one parent has taken against the other. Sometimes they are decided in cases brought by a local authority, or other child care agency, against one or both parents.

As a result, if a court has to decide, one of the parents may feel that he or she has lost and that the other has won. The loss may seem even more grievous if, because a parent has 'won', that parent then goes on to 'win' maintenance and possibly the former home for the child as well. So cases where parents are hostile and a court has to decide almost always end by fuelling the hostility. Inevitably, the children suffer even more.

So if you care anything for your children and even if you and your partner cannot agree anything else, you should try to agree arrangements for your children. So far as possible these arrangements have to take account of the realities of life and we will now turn to those realities, to what can be agreed, and to what a court may order if it is not agreed.

Section 8 of the 1989 Children Act substituted a new range of orders in place of the old custody and access orders which so long formed part of the picture affecting children:

1. *Residence orders* – which lay down where and with whom a child is to live.
2. *Contact orders* – which spell out who may have contact with a child and if necessary how, where, when and on what terms.
3. *Prohibited steps orders* – which may put restrictions on things which a person with parental responsibility for a child might otherwise be free to do – take a child abroad, for example.
4. *Specific issues orders* – which cover some particular interest of a child. For example, it has been suggested that a local authority might use such an order to secure needed medical treatment for a child in a case where its parents refused treatment.

Under Section 10 of the Act a parent, guardian or person who holds a residence order for a child may apply for any of these orders. With contact orders that list extends to include also:

(a) Step-parents
(b) Anyone with whom a child has lived for more than three years
(c) Anyone who has the consent of:
   • a person holding a residence order for the child, or
   • a local authority which has the child in its care, or
   • anyone else who has parental responsibility for the child.
(d) Anyone else covered by regulations made under the Act and to the extent spelled out in the regulations. Grandparents are perhaps the most important example in this category (see page 160).

Section 9 of the Act stipulates that unless they also qualify under one of the conditions previously stated, people who have been local authority foster parents must have the consent of the court or the local authority before they can apply for a Section 8 order relating to the fostered child.

Parental responsibility, residence, contact and guardianship

Parental responsibility and residence

Parental responsibility embraces the whole range of rights, duties, powers and responsibilities which a parent has or can have over a child and its property. Effectively, parental responsibility is the sum total of what married parents have with regard to their children when they are living happily together. But a person who does not have parental responsibility may still be legally liable to maintain a child (a man proved to be the father of a child who wants nothing to do with it, for example); and a person who, as a matter of fact, has care of a child may nevertheless do anything necessary to safeguard or protect its interests.[12]

The mother of a child automatically has parental responsibility for her child. So does its father if married to its mother when the child was born.[13] If the parents were not so married the father may acquire parental responsibility by agreement with the mother in a form laid down by regulations or by court order.[14] Parents with parental responsibility may appoint guardians for their children to act in the event of their death – by will or agreement in a form laid down by regulations.[15]

If a court makes a residence, contact, prohibited steps or specific order with regard to a child, that order effectively takes the matters covered by the order out of the general scope of parental responsibility. Those matters are then subject to the terms of the order and fall within the responsibility of the adults named in the order.[16]

Residence

If you started off as a family and your children came into that family, their first choice would almost always be to go on living with both of you. If you have reached the point where you and your partner cannot go on living together, that first choice is no longer available. But your children will still need a stable home, and if neither you nor your partner can provide one any longer, your local authority may provide one for them under either a voluntary or compulsory child care arrangement. In the majority of cases one of you at least can provide a home for them, even if that requires financial support from the other; both of you may want to, and the children will have to make their basic home with one of you only. The one they are to live with can obtain a residence order and if you cannot agree who they are to live with the court will decide.

Whoever is providing the home is likely to have to provide a home for all the children. Children need support from each other and only in the most extreme cases will a court ever consider splitting them between two parents.[17] That may still happen where there is a wide age gap and older children are so determined to stay with one parent that no court order is likely to make any difference. It may also happen when the family includes older children by a previous marriage or relationship of one of the parents, and younger children of both partners. Otherwise, however, the rule will almost always be the same for all of them.

In addition, if a court is asked, it is most unlikely to order that children split *time* equally between both parents. In one case parents originally agreed that their three-year-old daughter should live one week with father and one with mother. That arrangement lasted for five years before the mother called a halt to it. The Court of Appeal granted care and control to the mother with reasonable access to the father and said:

> 'The unusual order for joint care and control should never have been made. It was in the paramount interest of the child that, as she grew up and approached puberty, she should have a settled home in which there was some other female presence.'[18]

Any preference which a child expresses may be assessed and communicated to the court through the child welfare officer who, in contested cases at least, will almost always see the child at home beforehand. The court must listen to and respect sensible and mature views expressed by older children.[19]

The first thing which has to be decided is where and with whom your children are to live. If it is possible for you and your partner to agree that – still more, agree it without rancour – that may be one of the best things it is still in your power to do for your children. But if you cannot instinctively agree, it is still preferable to concede to what a court is likely to do than to take it to a fight. So it may help you to know the ways in which a court is likely to look at the residence problem:

1. The decision has to be made in the children's best interests as they stand at the time their destiny is decided, even though a different solution might in future years be appropriate.[20]
2. Children who have been in the sole care of either parent for a number of years are best staying with that parent[21] but, subject to that:
   (a) young children – and they seem to stay young until they finish at primary school – are best with their mother
   (b) female children of any age are best with their mother, so if you have daughters, their needs may decide the whole question.
3. Insofar as children express a preference, that is only likely to affect the issue if they are of an age to understand what is involved.[22]

In the nature of things most children end up in the primary care of their mother; fathers with such care are the exception. As to what may be exceptional, courts have given primary care to a father where a mother was judged to be mentally unstable and obsessed with a particular religious sect.[23] They have also given it where a daughter of 12 was absolutely adamant that she would not live with her mother.[24]

Contact

All arrangements and orders for children are essentially concerned with their interest, not with yours. That goes as much for contact orders as for any other. Adults may regard contact orders as giving them the right to see their children, much as they used to regard access orders. But the courts are concerned with the right of children to maintain contact with their parents and not the other way round. Why?

If children have regular contact with a parent, they have a pattern which they can use in growing up with a reasonably balanced and mature view of what being an adult of the sex of that parent is about. If they like the pattern, they may follow it; if they dislike it, they may avoid it. But either way it gives them a touchstone in their own development. Equally important, it is a touchstone whose quality changes with age. The young child who worships a parent, and becomes a teenager who loathes him – or her – may still evolve into a mature adult able to view both parents objectively. And if children end up thinking that their parents are not bad really, the chances are that their parents have done as well as any could. Similar principles apply when it comes to preserving contact between children and other people – grandparents, for example.

If your family has split up while this normal process is incomplete, your children still need to complete it. If they lose contact with one parent altogether, their perception of that parent will become frozen at the point where contact was lost, and it may affect their life – and yours – for years to come. For example, an 18-year-old girl was separated from her father when she was three. Her mother, who brought her up, made it clear that she had very little time for the father. But the girl remembered her father through the idolising eyes of a child of three. She searched for him, found him, and then abandoned both her mother and her career to go to live with him. He was not as bad as her mother had painted him, or as marvellous as the daughter imagined him, but she could not even begin to find that out until she was 18, and her father was then faced with accepting her into his family while she belatedly discovered reality. Her mother lost out altogether.

If your children are to have the best chance of surviving the collapse of your relationship, they will need to be able to see the parent who no longer lives with them often, and free of anxiety that the parent they are living with minds. If it is possible for the arrangements to be flexible, so much the better. But, flexible or not, fixed arrangements should be observed with a religious respect. If you tell your children you are coming to see them, they will be waiting for you and will suffer more if you are late or do not turn up than if you had not bothered. And if you know your children are expecting your former partner, and you arrange for them to do something else, equally you harm them.

The children's need and right to maintain contact with a parent with whom they do not reside is likely to be respected and ordered in every case where there is an established relationship between parent and child, unless the characteristics of the parent are such that it is not in the child's interest.

So, for example, contact has been refused in cases where there was a clear risk of violence between parent and child: in some cases where the parent has been suffering from an illness, particularly a mental illness, which might disturb the child seriously apart from any risk; and in many cases where the parents separated, if they ever lived together, before any relationship developed between father and child. But because it is now understood that children need to know who their parents are, and to have contact with them, the courts are increasingly likely to allow parents who wish to establish or maintain links with their children to do so, even if links have previously been tenuous.[25]

A contact order may do no more than allow reasonable contact, leaving it to the parents to agree how it shall be worked out. But if they cannot agree, either may apply to the court to define contact, and, failing all else, a court will define it in terms of hours, days and if needs be dates, and may then or thereafter order that access be supervised by a child welfare officer.

Beyond that, however, there is very little that the courts can do to enforce contact arrangements against a parent who is determined to obstruct them, heedless of the children's interest. Sadly, such parents are not uncommon.

In theory a court might make non-compliance with its orders a matter of contempt of court, for which a parent might then be committed to prison.[26] But in practice this is virtually impossible if the court is to keep its eye firmly on the interests of the children, as it must: after all, what effect is it likely to have on the children if the court sends mother to prison for contempt and father appears on the court papers which say who applied to send her there?

Hypothetically, a court might take the view that if a parent persistently wrecks contact, that is the clearest possible evidence that the wrecker was wrongly left care of the children in the first place. If it did, it might then be prepared to vary the basic order if the other parent applied for residence. But if any application on this basis has been attempted, no court has so far been reported as willing to grant it. And since disturbing the established lives of the children is always considered undesirable, reversing established residence arrangements is inevitably unlikely unless the parents agree.

Court applications

The large majority of court applications over children combine automatically with divorce proceedings and the pattern of these proceedings has already been outlined. But the court can consider all aspects of children's cases either in cases brought exclusively for that purpose, or in conjunction with proceedings for maintenance and separation, rather than divorce, between the parents.

So, for example, both Family Proceedings and County Courts can consider applications for children's orders. These courts can also consider applications by grandparents for contact with grandchildren, applications by third parties for adoption, and applications for orders by local authorities and others concerned with child care. Finally, the Family Division of the High Court which has even wider powers can include provisions on any of these issues on any order made in wardship proceedings.

This introduces another set of possible child-related proceedings, so a note on each may help you.

Grandparents, guardians, adoption, local authorities and wards of court

Access by grandparents

A grandparent may apply to the court for contact with a grandchild.[27] Such applications may be granted in any case where the court is satisfied that contact is in the interest of the child. That is particularly likely to be the case where:

(a) the parent who was child of the grandparents has died, disappeared, or for some other reason is not available to exercise his or her own rights, or

(b) there is a relationship already established between grandparents and child.

Grandparents cannot apply for contact where a child is in the care of a local authority. And grandparents who are not able to see their grandchildren because their own child will not allow it should not imagine that the law necessarily gives them a back-door right to change a situation which flows from the fragility of their own family relationships. As in all child cases the child comes first, and a court may not take the view that it is in the child's interest to override a parent's wishes in favour of that parent's parents.

Guardianship

Under Sections 5 and 6 of the 1989 Children Act parents with parental responsibility may appoint a guardian for their children to act in the event of their death – by will or agreement in prescribed form. A court may also appoint as guardian any individual who applies if no one has parental responsibility for the child, or if a parent or guardian who had a residence order has died. Once appointed a guardian has parental responsibility and may apply for a residence, contact or other order which a court may make for a child's welfare.

Adoption

If a child is legally adopted, it becomes the child of the parents who adopt it for all legal purposes. Once it has reached the age of 18, however, it may apply to the Registrar General for a copy of its original birth certificate[28] and is entitled to have that certificate after receiving compulsory counselling. The adopted child may then, if it wishes, use the information in its birth certificate to trace, or to attempt to trace, its natural parents. The office of the Registrar General which deals with these matters[29] will now, by concession, note any natural relatives' wishes about future contact on the records of an adopted person. That information (but no other apart from the original birth certificate) may be passed on in the course of counselling to anyone who asks for his or her original birth certificate.

We all need to know who we are and where we came from – it is an essential part of our own identity. So any parent who adopts a child – or gives one up for adoption – must be prepared for that child to pursue that curiosity in due course, however successful the adoptive relationship may be.

Basically, both parents, if they survive and are known, must be notified of any application for adoption and must consent to it, although the courts have power to dispense with consent if satisfied that it has been withheld unreasonably. But the test of reasonableness is whether the parent possesses the insight to make the judgements of a reasonable parent, though the fact that a mother keeps changing her mind may not be regarded as unreasonable.[30]

A parent may adopt his or her own child – in times past that was common when women were not married and wished to try to spare themselves and their children the embarrassment of explanations of illegitimacy, and sometimes to exclude natural fathers. That sort of application is becoming less common and is likely to be even rarer now that the Family Law Reform Act 1987 has swept away the legal distinctions between children of married and unmarried relationships. Otherwise, however, only married couples can apply for adoption and any adoption order made in favour of an unmarried couple is void.[31]

The recognition that children need to know their true identity, reflected in the right of adopted children to obtain their original birth certificates, now makes it unlikely that adoption will be permitted by a parent and step-parent after remarriage, even when the other natural parent consents.[32] And while such adoptions may be allowed when the other natural parent has died, disappeared, or never had any established parent–child relationship with the child, a mother–stepfather adoption order has been revoked, on the application of grandparents, who had always had a close relationship with the child.[33]

In rare cases it may be judged that it is in the child's interest that an adoption order includes an order for continuing access with a child's natural parents or family, but that will only be done in the most exceptional case if the adopting parents do not agree.[34]

Adoptions which involve children who are strangers to the adopting parents now all flow through recognised adoption agencies or local authority care departments, and where they are involved they will give full guidance on the procedures involved. Though both County and magistrates Family Proceedings courts deal with adoption applications, you are likely to find magistrates court procedure simpler if making an adoption application without help from a solicitor in a case which does not involve such an agency.

Local authority care

Local councils have a legal duty to promote the welfare of the children in their area[35] and this includes a duty to provide full-time care for them if no other appropriate person can or will. When children are accepted or taken into care they will be placed with suitable foster parents if such can be found. Otherwise, they will be taken into a local authority children's home or similar institution.

Local authority care can be an entirely voluntary matter – a parent who is not able, perhaps only for a short period, to cope with the care of children, may ask his or her authority to provide such care. But if a voluntary care arrangement continues for some time, the child's needs for stability may begin to override the parent's right to reclaim the child and the parent may then face a compulsory care application by the local authority, or a residence application by established foster parents.

Local authorities, police officers or other authorised persons may also start proceedings in a magistrates Family Proceedings court for a compulsory care order. If such an order is made, the local authority has the right to the general care of the child, to the exclusion of the parents.

Compulsory care applications[36] can be made where a child is suffering or likely to suffer significant harm, and the harm or its likelihood is attributable to:

(a) the care which the child is receiving or is likely to receive not being what it would be reasonable to expect a parent to give, or

(b) the child being beyond parental control.

A care order does not necessarily involve taking a child away from its family. In appropriate cases (persistent truancy, for example) parents may be offered the option, under financial penalty, of making sure that the child toes the line, and children may be placed under the watchful eye of a social worker under a supervision order. If a child is removed from the care of its parents, it may be committed into the care of a guardian named in a guardianship order, the local authority, or a hospital if it is mentally ill. If a child is taken out of the care of its parents, both or either of them may have to pay Child Support and possibly court maintenance on top.

Wide powers exist to deal with emergencies. Anyone can apply to a Family Proceedings (magistrates) court for an emergency protection order under which a child may be removed from its home to an approved safe place.[37] If a police officer considers that a child is at risk of significant harm he can immediately remove the child to a suitable place and put him under police protection.[38]

A child may not be detained for more than a maximum period of eight days under these emergency procedures; and if, after they have elapsed, a local authority does not start full care proceedings within that time the child must be returned to its home. As a result of the Cleveland child abuse cases the 1989 Children Act has substantially strengthened both children's and parents' rights in these cases.

Wardship and child abduction

Wardship has the longest history of all legal child care proceedings. Originally, however, it was hardly benevolent. In feudal England the Crown had financial claims when property passed on inheritance, and a financial interest in the property and marriage prospects of people who inherited when under age. Ever careful of its own, the Crown ensured that children under 21 with such prospects came under the care of the Lord Chancellor as Wards in Chancery, and it is from that inauspicious beginning that the modern child care aspects of wardship evolved.

As a result of all the other alternatives now available wardship is largely irrelevant, and serves only as a final long-stop if nothing else will do. In particular, only parents and other individuals concerned about a child's welfare can now apply for wardship. Local authorities have to use the statutory care proceedings.

A child becomes a ward of court immediately someone appears before a High Court judge – anywhere – with a summons and the judge orders that the child becomes a ward of court. Anyone else concerned need only be served with notice of the proceedings after the initial order is made. And while wardship lapses if an application is not made for a hearing date within 21 days of the original order, the child otherwise remains a ward of court until the summons is heard.

So long as a child is a ward, its destiny is wholly in the hands of the Family Division of the High Court. So, for example, the court can order a parent to pay or contribute towards the child's maintenance; it can order the immediate arrest of anyone who wrongly has possession of the child; its officers can take action to prevent the child being taken out of the country; and if the child has been taken out of the country, the court can order steps which may compel its return. In one case where an author had absconded across the Atlantic with his children, the court sequestrated all his royalties so that he was penniless when he landed in America and had no choice but to return.

In time past, wardship was frequently used by rich parents who wished to stop their daughters marrying people considered undesirable. In more modern times it has been used more commonly to stop parents snatching children from those who legally had their care. It has also been used to obtain authority from the court for medical treatment in cases where, for one reason or another, no other authority would do or was available.

Wardship remains useful, particularly in cases where property is involved, since magistrates cannot deal with that.

The physical care of children is now covered by local authority child care responsibilities; and since the 1984 Child Abduction Acts, it has become a criminal offence (enforceable internationally by treaty) for any parent or guardian to take a child out of the country without the consent of every parent, guardian and any other person who has parental responsibility, or a residence order. Kidnapping by a parent is therefore now a crime. If you are concerned about the disappearance of a child in your care, you now need only go to your local police station to call up all the help – police search, arrest and stop orders on ports and airports – which previously could only be summoned through wardship proceedings.

Notes

1. The property and inheritance rules under the 1987 Act came into force on 3 March 1988
2. Section 19(4) Family Law Reform Act 1987 (FLRA)
3. Section 4 Children Act 1989 (CA)
4. Paragraph 2, 1st Schedule CA
5. Section 4 CA
6. Sections 24 and 25 FLRA
7. Section 22 FLRA
8. Section 29 FLRA
9. *McV* v *B* (1987) *The Times* 28 November
10. Section 27 FLRA
11. Section 1 CA
12. Section 3 CA
13. Section 2 CA
14. Section 4 CA
15. Section 5 CA
16. Section 8 CA
17. *R* v *R* (1986) *The Times* 28 May
18. *C* v *C* (1988) *The Times* 1 February
19. In Re *P* (a minor) (1991) *The Times* 10 October
20. *T* v *T* (1986) *The Times* 4 August
21. *B* v *B* (1972) *The Times* 29 November
22. *M* v *M* (1987) *The Times* 3 January; and see note 19 above
23. *T* v *T* (1974) *The Times* 2 July
24. See note 22 above
25. In Re *C* (minors' parental rights) (1991) *The Times* 8 August; in Re *M* (minors) *The Times* 22 February
26. *D* v *D* (1990) *The Times* 16 November
27. Section 10 CA
28. Section 20 Adoption Act 1976; Schedule 10 CA
29. General Register Office, Segensworth Road, Titchfield, Fareham, Hants PO15 5RR
30. In Re *P* (an infant) (1984) *The Times* 19 May
31. In Re *R* & *A* (minors) (1974) *The Times* 11 June
32. See in Re a minor (1976) *The Times* 26 November
33. In Re *LA* (a minor) (1978) *The Times* 27 April
34. In Re *M* (1985) *The Times* 9 May; in Re *C* (a minor) (1988) *The Times* 26 February

Splitting Up

Chapter 11

Professional Advice, Costs, Legal Aid and Complaints

Legal advice or do it yourself?

If you wanted to discover *all* the law on the topics covered in this book you would need to read more than 15,000 pages of professional text. Even solicitors, barristers – and accountants in their field – do not know all the law; but their training and experience give them an instinct for the existence of relevant legal provisions sufficient to send them looking for them when specific problems prompt it. As in many fields of life, it is usually more important to recognise that a problem exists than it is, immediately, to know the answer. The professional has a trained instinct for this and, quite simply, if you do not have the training, you are not likely to have the instinct.

So in an ideal world this book would consist only of one sentence: 'If you have problems with your family relationships go to see a solicitor.'

But we do not live in an ideal world. Even if you have passed your affairs over to a solicitor lock, stock and barrel, he, living in his professional world, may assume that matters which are entirely clear to him are equally clear to you – and they may not be. In addition, he may well be so overwhelmed by the pressures of attempting to complete all his clients' work that he never has time to explain the situation adequately to you. And sometimes, dare one say it, he may know what has to be done without totally understanding it himself. So even if you have a solicitor, a book such as this, designed to give a bird's eye view of the main problems, should allow you a little more peace by giving you the general picture.

It goes beyond that, however. The cost of professional help is formidable, particularly if you are going to have to meet it out of only a portion of the resources previously available to you. When relationships break down that is almost always the case. So anything you can do yourself, and anything which you and your partner can agree, may have a substantial value. If it has, you, your partner and any children will all be better off.

In simple cases you may be able to do the lot yourselves; the procedures for undefended divorce are already designed to make that relatively easy. But in all family matters there are things which you can do to limit the burden of costs.

More than anything else it is failure to agree – particularly over children and financial matters – which sends costs soaring. The real costs start rolling in when each of you has solicitors exchanging letters, copy documents, telephone calls, requests for information, copies of that information, affidavits setting out that information, court summonses for information, and court summonses for hearings, and then spending even more time going to the court for the hearings as well. Yet the whole object of these formidably costly procedures is no more than to establish precisely:

1. What income and capital each of you has.
2. How, if at all, it should be reallocated between you now that the relationship in which you previously enjoyed it has fallen apart.
3. By whom and how any children should be cared for.

And that is why so much of this book is devoted to these problems. If you and your partner can reach agreement on these to your reasonable mutual satisfaction, you immediately cut away the main part of the cancer of costs.

If you reach agreement, you will still be wise to ask a solicitor to draw up and deal with the court summons for a consent order to put the court seal of approval on what you have decided. The court order has to be right and has to cover many legal contingencies, some of which have been discussed, in precise and accurate legal words. But if you rigorously limit your instructions to your solicitor to that, and that is all your solicitor has to do, costs for that exercise should be minimal.

In most cases it will still be sensible to have a solicitor. But where humanly possible confine his instructions strictly to implementing measures which you have yourselves agreed. Admittedly, having a solicitor almost certainly means that both of you must have one. One solicitor cannot (yet) act for both of you and a court may be reluctant to implement even agreed deals if one of you has not been near a solicitor at all. But so long as both of you remain equally resolute in your instructions, that is not likely to overcomplicate the position.

Choosing a solicitor and working with him

Choosing a solicitor

One of the commonest requests from people whose relationships are crumbling is for the name of a *good* solicitor. They may never have consulted a solicitor before, or, for a variety of reasons, they may now need a different one. For example, family solicitors who know both parties usually conclude that they cannot fairly act for either against the other.

Many people – friends, relations and professional people generally (including family solicitors) – have established contacts with solicitors and can make a personal recommendation. So, often, can general advisory agencies like the Citizens Advice Bureau. And on the whole a personal recommendation is likely to be the most reliable.

But remember that family law work is a mainstream activity for virtually all solicitors. How could it be otherwise when divorce petitions alone now average 180,000 a year? So most firms of solicitors have one or more people who are both qualified and experienced in family law work: in some, particularly the larger ones with a number of partners, there are people who do nothing else. So do not imagine that there is some select band of experts, hidden away, whose skills are so overpowering that they are likely to make any profound difference to the outcome of your particular case.

In the highly technical and specialised field of child care the Law Society now maintains a list of solicitors who are considered to have appropriate qualifications, and the names of people on that list can be obtained from the Law Society.[1] A number of solicitors active in family law work are also members of the voluntary Solicitors Family Law Association (SFLA) and again you can establish contact with them through the Law Society. But while membership of the SFLA is likely to mean that a solicitor is much engaged in family law work, the fact that he is not a member does not imply the opposite.

The chances are that you will be reasonably served by any firm of solicitors which is prepared to accept you as a client, and will be recommended by them to another solicitor if they cannot help you. Failing all else, therefore, do not be afraid to walk through the door of the first solicitor's office you come to.

Working with a solicitor

In family law work you pay your solicitor, sometimes with help from legal aid, for the work he has to do and particularly for the time he has to spend doing it. So the more organised you can be before you see him, and as often as you see him, the better.

If you want him to prepare proceedings for maintenance, divorce or separation and particularly if you are considering proceedings which involve allegations of your spouse's unreasonable behaviour, write out (preferably type out) all the details of your case beforehand, Start off with full details of the people involved – full names, addresses and dates of birth of all adults and children involved; if married, take a copy of your marriage certificate along if you have it, and give the date and place of marriage even if you do not. Give the date – exact or approximate – of all specific events which have a bearing on your case and set them out in chronological order. That alone can save an hour – maybe more.

Prepare a complete statement setting out all your income from every source, and include details of the tax, superannuation or pension, mortgage interest, National Insurance and other deductions which come out of it. If possible, attach details of your income certified by your employer or inspector of taxes, copy tax returns and assessments if they are available, and provide copies of your accounts for the last three years if you are self-employed. List full details of all the property you own whether in your own name, or jointly with others, and of all mortgages and debts. As far as you can, give the same details for your partner and children.

If your solicitor asks for information, provide it as quickly as you can. And when you communicate with him write rather than use the telephone whenever possible: telephone messages too often go adrift or are forgotten.

If you ask for advice, do not then start arguing about it because you do not like it. There's no point in having a dog and barking yourself; and, whether or not it is true, your solicitor is likely to conclude that if you knew the answer yourself you would not have consulted him.

But if you have serious reservations about the advice you have received, and have a specific reason, do not be afraid to explain that reason to your solicitor or to invite his comment. If something which seems relevant to your problem has been mentioned in a newspaper or on radio or television, for example, it is entirely possible that you noted it and he did not. But remember that it is equally possible that you may have misinterpreted what you read, saw or heard, and that while it may be wise to mention it, it is rarely wise to base an argument on it. Remember, too, that you can always ask your solicitor to refer any particular point to a barrister (counsel) for a second opinion, or indeed that you can ask another solicitor for his. But remember also that you may have to pay for it.

Finally, do not expect precise and definite guidance from your solicitor on the issues which probably matter most – the destiny of your children, income and property. For the reasons discussed in many passages of this book he cannot give them and, frankly, if he tries, you should be cautious of the answers. He may, of course, know from his own experience how the courts in which he usually appears deal with cases such as yours; so his crystal-gazing may be more accurate and well informed if your case is to go into one of those courts. But if it is not, or if your partner does not have a solicitor with the same knowledge and experience, variations in practice are still likely to leave a yawning gap between the positions which different individuals may consider appropriate.

Solicitors' costs and legal aid

Costs

Rarely, if ever, is it possible at the beginning of any family law case to know how much work will have to be done before it is concluded. So your ultimate bill will depend on the work which your solicitor has to do and most of it will be measured on the time which it takes to do it. Under rules made in 1990 your solicitor should give you the best information he can about the costs he is likely to have to charge you when you first consult him. If the work is such that he cannot quote a fixed fee he ought to give you details of how his costs will be calculated. Unless you have a legal aid certificate your solicitor will almost certainly require you to pay him in advance a sum (or sums by instalments) on account of the costs which will arise on your case, and he may also bill you periodically as the work progresses. He is not under any obligation to go on working for you if you do not comply with cost arrangements.

Seldom, if ever, is it possible to predict in advance how much work will have to be done in family matters. So, fixed court fees and expenses apart, the only cost information a solicitor is likely to be able to give you in advance will mostly consist of the hourly rates which he will have to charge. Normally, such quotations include different rates for different levels of legal qualification. Work done by partners will cost more than work done by assistant solicitors. Work done by assistant solicitors may cost more than work done by legal executives or articled or other clerks.

Time is usually measured by the time of the person actually doing the work – the fee-earner – and the cost of supporting staff and services (typists, ordinary clerks, rent, rates and all other overhead costs) is built into fee-earners' hourly rates by averaging the total overhead costs out between all fee-earners.

Inevitably, the size and location of the firm have a bearing on its overheads and on the hourly rates which it will hope to charge. For example, rates between £150 and £400 an *hour* have been reported for family law work in some of the largest firms of solicitors in London, and since such rates are wildly beyond anything which can usually be recovered on legal aid work, firms who have to charge them simply do not accept legally aided clients.

But even legal aid rates, which are such that an increasing number of solicitors are finding that they must abandon legally aided work altogether, should suffice to give you pause for thought. General County Court matrimonial work is costed at £3.60 each for letters written and telephone calls made; £1.80 for letters received; and from £38.20 to £40.25 per hour (depending on district) for time otherwise spent plus 50 per cent of the total. So the effective hourly rate is approximately £60 an hour (figures fixed in 1991 and still applicable in 1994).

Why are hourly rates so high? Legal work is labour-intensive, and the skills required make that labour very costly. Other overheads apart, staff wages may absorb 60 per cent or more of every pound which a solicitors' firm charges. Relatively, the cost of supplies which are essential whoever does the work – paper, equipment, heating, lighting and other such overheads – is only a small fraction of a solicitor's overall costs. This is why doing it yourself – wherever that is possible – offers such substantial savings: the time you save cuts into the most costly part of the whole job, which is also subject to VAT.

Apart from your solicitor's own charges you will also have to pay any specific sums of money which he has to pay out on your case. So if expenses have to be incurred for counsel, court fees, expert witnesses, Stamp Duty, property searches or anything else, the cost of these will be added.

At the end of the day you can, if you wish, challenge your solicitor's bill. You can indeed require him to submit a detailed bill in specialised form for adjudication by a court Registrar or taxing master through the process of taxation described in Chapter 2. If your solicitor has quoted an hourly charging rate at the outset, that will be persuasive of the hourly rates which the court should consider, but not necessarily conclusive. If no hourly rate has been quoted, the court will work on what it considers to be generally acceptable hourly rates in the vicinity plus a percentage mark-up – and it may be 50 per cent or more – geared to the complexity and difficulty of the case.

It may be that if you have 'won' your case, your partner will be ordered to pay your costs. If such an order is made, the court may fix the amount of costs. If it does not and if the costs cannot be agreed, the amount recoverable will again be decided by the process of taxation. But, apart from cases under the Inheritance (Provision for Family & Dependants) Act 1975, where costs tend to be ordered out of the estate, costs orders are increasingly rare in family law cases. One reason is that their consequence may utterly disrupt the effect of the property and maintenance orders which the court has made. The chances are, therefore, that in the absence of any agreement about costs, each party will be left paying his or her own.

In addition, there are hidden snags in a costs order. An ordinary costs order is not likely to result in anything like full recovery of your costs. If you are awarded costs on an indemnity basis, it may do, but the chances are that there will still be some costs which you will have to pay. In addition, you will have to pay them anyway, if, and to the extent that, the costs cannot actually be recovered from the person ordered to pay them. On the whole, people who have lost family dispute cases and have been ordered to pay their partner's costs are even more likely to try to avoid the bill than in the general run of debts. And if they have no steady employment or available property – which often follows family law decisions – recovering costs by further legal proceedings may be impossible.

The State legal aid system

Solicitors have a professional duty to advise you about the State system so you should not be afraid to make an enquiry as to whether you qualify your first question. Where legal aid is a possibility you are only covered by legal aid from the time it is granted, and may be billed by your solicitor for work done before then. That also gives legal aid questions a high priority. We are concerned in family cases, incidentally, with legal aid in civil, not criminal proceedings.

There are two branches to legal aid:

1. Legal advice under the Legal Advice (Green Form) Scheme which

may also be extended to a sort of half-way house in court cases –
legal assistance by way of representation.

2. Legal aid with court cases.

To qualify for either you first have to satisfy a means test, and the
means tests are not the same for both. But because both are means
tested, remember that any change in your circumstances, even a
change resulting from the outcome of advice or proceedings, may
affect your right to legal aid. And there is a vital preliminary warning:

**Legal aid is essentially in the nature of a loan. If you are legally
aided and recover or preserve anything of value (even your own
house) the Legal Aid Fund has first claim on whatever is recovered
or preserved for costs. To the extent that the Legal Aid Fund ends
up paying anything to your solicitor it can claw back what it has
paid from your winnings. If your house, or money to buy one, is
what you win you will not then have to sell the house to pay the
costs. The debt can be carried over until the house is sold, and
maybe until a replacement house is sold. But you will have to pay
interest on the debt, as on any mortgage debt, until it is repaid. If
legal aid is granted, the Legal Aid Fund will cover your solicitor's
costs through to the conclusion of the proceedings covered by the
legal aid certificate so you do not have to worry about that. But do
not imagine that you can forget about costs altogether – if you end
up with anything, you may still have to pay. And if you are ordered
to pay the costs of your opponent those must be paid by you anyway.**

Now to the mechanics.

Legal advice

Legal advice is dealt with by solicitors. They have a standard
simplified means test formula (based on the Green Form which has
given State-aided legal advice its colloquial name) which allows them
to calculate very quickly whether you qualify, and what contribution,
if any, you have to pay. If you qualify for legal advice on a means basis,
a solicitor can advise you about most matters which may arise in
family cases, but there is a financial limit. As at 1994 the limit covers
three hours' preparatory work if you are petitioning for divorce, and
two hours' in any other case. In appropriate cases he can apply to have
that limit extended by the regional Legal Aid Office. As the procedure
is simple, and as the figures change fairly frequently, the simple

answer, if you hope to qualify for free or assisted legal advice, is to ask a solicitor.

Legal aid

Legal aid covers your own solicitor's costs for legal proceedings defined in the legal aid certificate. It is available for matters involving maintenance, property and children – in the magistrates, County and High Courts as appropriate but not for undefended divorce proceedings (ie the procedure for obtaining the divorce alone) nor is it normally granted to allow anyone to defend divorce proceedings.

Most solicitors and many Citizens Advice Bureaux stock legal aid application forms and can supply them to you. These require considerable detail and, while solicitors do not have to help you fill them in, they usually will and may do so as part of Green Form work where a Green Form certificate has already been issued.

Your right to legal aid depends on two factors:

1. Having what, on the face of it, is a legal right to pursue in court proceedings. This is judged by experienced lawyers employed by the Legal Aid Board. Because of the nature of family law proceedings it is comparatively rare to find a case where such a right does not exist.
2. Satisfying a means test which is very much more complicated than that used for the Green Form Scheme and on which DSS officers may make detailed enquiries.

Delays may ensue between making a legal aid application and receiving the result. Both legal aid and DSS staffs dealing with these applications are heavily overloaded. If, however, legal action is urgent, an application can be made for an *emergency legal aid certificate* to cover it, although if you are granted an emergency certificate, you will have to undertake to repay any costs advanced if, in the end, it is found that your means did not qualify you for legal aid.

If your means are very limited – typically, if you are already receiving DSS Income or Family Support – you may be granted legal aid without any financial contribution and in that case the certificate will be issued without any prior offer to you. Since the DSS deal with applications for Income and Family Support far more quickly than applications for legal aid you may be wise to apply for these first if you think you qualify. If your right to these is established, it will help to speed your legal aid application.

If you are of more substantial means (or if your partner controls most of what you have and you have relatively little) you may still qualify for legal aid, but may have to contribute to your costs. In considering these questions the Legal Aid Board will take into account your income, your capital, your dependants and your available resources, and the only simple guidance on whether or not you qualify is to apply and see.

If legal aid is available, but the Legal Aid Board consider that you should pay a contribution, you will receive an offer of legal aid which spells out the contributions. You will not be issued with a legal aid certificate, and so will not be able to take steps covered by it, until you have signed and returned your acceptance. You do not, of course, have to accept the offer but, if you refuse it, you will not be granted legal aid and will have to cover the costs of your case yourself or abandon it.

Once granted a legal aid certificate guarantees payment to your solicitor for all the work which he has to do to complete the matters covered by the certificate.

A legal aid certificate may be limited to certain preliminary steps – obtaining evidence from witnesses and the advice of counsel, for example. If a certificate is limited, it will not be extended until these steps are complete, or even then if they reveal that you have no case on which to proceed. Alternatively, and more commonly in family proceedings, it will cover all the essential steps up to the conclusion of those proceedings. If the certificate does not cover all the work which your solicitor has to do, however, he can apply on your behalf for it to be extended. And where that is necessary it is obviously in his interest to do so or he may not be paid for any extra work he does.

At the end of the day your solicitor will usually (for the same reason) remember to ask the court to order that his costs against the Legal Aid Board be taxed by the court, and those costs will also include the expenses incurred in dealing with the case. Taxation may itself take a number of months but once it is concluded the Legal Aid Board will pay your solicitor and any barrister the figures fixed by the court. As already emphasised the Legal Aid Board will then reclaim from anything you have ended up with any balance not covered by your previous contributions and costs *actually recovered* from your opponent.

You have one concession, previously noted. If you have recovered or retained your house, or been awarded money to buy one, you will not then be compelled to sell it to pay legal aid costs. Instead, the Legal Aid Board will place a charge – equivalent to a mortgage – on your property to secure payment of the costs when the property (or sometimes a replacement of it) is sold. But as with any mortgage you have to pay interest on the costs until the Legal Aid Board receives them.

Complaints against solicitors

We have already discussed your right to challenge the amount of costs by requiring your solicitor to have them taxed by the court. The amount of costs, however, is not the only issue which may give rise to a sense of grievance between client and solicitor.

There certainly are cases where complaint is warranted. But before we deal finally with that, cautions are again appropriate.

Disenchantment with one's solicitor is more common in family proceedings than in virtually any other. Indeed, some solicitors say the best way to lose a client for ever is to act for him or her in divorce proceedings.

Your relationship with your solicitor is potentially at risk from the start. You are likely to be disenchanted with your former partner and so with anyone who fails to deliver what you expect out of the wreckage. If your solicitor is doing his job properly, he will have to advise you about the realities of your case as he sees them, even though he knows that the advice may not be welcome. But a significant number of people feel like shooting the messenger merely because they do not like the message.

Again, the law and its procedures do not help. You want precise advice and the law does not contain the basis for it. You want a predictable timetable and the procedural rules only put a very wide frame round it. You are accustomed to dealing with everything immediately – perhaps your solicitor is too. But the expedition and efficiency with which your case is ultimately dealt will be the lowest common denominator of all involved – you, your solicitor, your former partner's solicitor, your former partner, the courts and so on. Any one of them can make a long, tedious and expensive business even longer, more tedious and more expensive.

If, however, you have pinpointed your solicitor as the author of real misfortune, there are several steps you can take. If he has missed something which, professionally, he should not have missed and you have suffered loss which can be measured in financial terms, you may be able to recover damages against him for negligence. All solicitors compulsorily carry insurance cover against this risk, for every solicitor knows that however hard he tries, sooner or later he may get something wrong. To pursue a negligence claim, however, you will almost certainly need a new solicitor to help you. Your local law society (listed in the telephone directory) should be able to give you the name of a solicitor in your area nominated to deal with such cases if you cannot immediately find one yourself. The Law Society in London will also provide names and addresses if necessary.

But you may have problems other than straightforward negligence. The Solicitors Complaints Bureau (SCB)[2] may be able to help you with these.

The following are within the scope of the SCB:

(a) delay in answering letters or in dealing with your case generally
(b) any failure to deal properly with your money – bear in mind, for example, that by regulation solicitors are supposed to credit their clients with interest if they hold sizeable sums of clients' money for very long
(c) acting for both parties in a case where their interests conflict
(d) overcharging, dishonesty or deception
(e) failure to return your papers to you if you have asked for them and have paid all outstanding costs
(f) shoddy work – a solicitor may be ordered to rectify mistakes and his costs may be reduced.

If in doubt write with full details of your problem to the SCB and ask it to channel you into the right slot.

Notes

1. The Law Society, 113 Chancery Lane, London WC2A 1PL
2. The Solicitors Complaints Bureau, Victoria Court, 8 Dormer Place, Leamington Spa, Warwickshire CV32 5AE; 01926 820082

Text of Sections 22 to 25A of the Matrimonial Causes Act 1973 as Subsequently Amended

Note. Section 22 deals with temporary maintenance which may be ordered during the course of proceedings; Section 23 defines the types of maintenance and lump sum orders which a court may make; Section 24 defines the courts' power to order a transfer of property; and Section 24A their powers to order a sale of property where that is appropriate to allow parties to be paid out their shares. Finally, Section 25 defines the criteria which the courts must apply in considering any financial order and Section 25A deals with the power to end maintenance – the clean break.

22 Maintenance pending suit

On a petition for divorce, nullity of marriage or judicial separation, the court may make an order for maintenance pending suit, that is to say, an order requiring either party to the marriage to make to the other such periodical payments for his or her maintenance and for such term, being a term beginning not earlier than the date of the presentation of the petition and ending with the date of the determination of the suit, as the court thinks reasonable.

23 Financial provision orders in connection with divorce proceedings, etc

(1) On granting a decree of divorce, a decree of nullity of marriage or a decree of judicial separation or at any time thereafter (whether, in the case of a decree of divorce or of nullity of marriage, before or after the decree is made absolute), the court may make any one of the following orders, that is to say:

(a) an order that either party to the marriage shall make to the other such periodical payments, for such term, as may be specified in the order;

(b) an order that either party to the marriage shall secure to the other to the satisfaction of the court such periodical payments, for such term, as may be so specified;

(c) an order that either party to the marriage shall pay to the other such lump sum or sums as may be so specified;

(d) an order that a party to the marriage shall make to such a person as may be specified in the order for the benefit of a child of the family, or to such a child, such periodical payments, for such term, as may be so specified;

(e) an order that a party to the marriage shall secure to such person as may be so specified for the benefit of such a child, or to such a child, to the satisfaction of the court, such periodical payments, for such term, as may be so specified;

(f) an order that a party to the marriage shall pay to such person as may be so specified for the benefit of such a child, or to such a child, such lump sum as may be so specified;

subject however, in the case of an order under paragraph (d), (e) or (f) above, the restrictions imposed by Section 29(1) and (3) below on the making of financial provision orders in favour of children who have attained the age of 18.

(2) The court may also, subject to those restrictions, make any one or more of the orders mentioned in subsection (1)(d), (e) and (f) above:

(a) in any proceedings for divorce, nullity of marriage or judicial separation, before granting a decree; and

(b) where any such proceedings are dismissed after the beginning of the trial, either forthwith or within a reasonable period after the dismissal.

(3) Without prejudice to the generality of subsection (1)(c) or (f) above:

(a) an order under this section that a party to a marriage shall pay a lump sum to the other party may be made for the purpose of enabling that other party to meet any liabilities or expenses reasonably incurred by him or her in maintaining himself or herself or any child of the family before making an application for an order under this section in his or her favour;

(b) an order under this section for the payment of a lump sum to or for the benefit of a child of the family be made for the purpose of enabling any liabilities or expenses reasonably incurred by or for the benefit of that child before the making of an application for an order under this section in his favour to be met; and

(c) an order under this section for the payment of a lump sum may provide for the payment of that sum by instalments of such amounts as may be specified in the order and may require the payment of the instalments to be secured to the satisfaction of the court.

(4) The power of the court under subsection (1) or (2)(a) above to make an order in favour of a child of the family shall be exercisable from time to time; and where the court makes an order in favour of a child under subsection (2)(b) above, it may from time to time, subject to the restrictions mentioned in subsection (1) above, make a further order in his favour of any of the kinds mentioned in subsection (1)(d), (e) or (f) above.

(5) Without prejudice to the power to give a direction under Section 30 below for the settlement of an instrument by conveyancing counsel, where an order is made under subsection (1)(a), (b) or (c) above on or after granting a decree of divorce or nullity of marriage, neither the order nor any settlement made in pursuance of the order shall take effect unless the decree has been made absolute.

(6) Where the court:

(a) makes an order under this section for the payment of a lump sum; and

(b) directs:

(i) that payment of the sum or any part of it shall be deferred; or

(ii) that the sum or any part of it shall be paid by instalments, the court may order that the amount deferred or the instalments shall carry interest at such rate as may be specified by the order from such date, not earlier than the date of the order, as may be so specified, until the date when payment of it is due.

24 Property adjustment orders in connection with divorce proceedings, etc

(1) On granting a decree of divorce, a decree of nullity of marriage or a decree of judicial separation or at any time thereafter (whether, in the case of a decree of divorce or of nullity of marriage, before or after the decree is made absolute), the court may make one or more of the following orders, that is to say:

(a) an order that a party to the marriage shall transfer to the other party, to any child of the family or to such person as may be specified in the order for the benefit of such a child such property as may be so specified, being property to which the first-mentioned party is entitled, either in possession or reversion;

(b) an order that a settlement of such property as may be so specified, being property to which a party to the marriage is so entitled, be made to the satisfaction of the court for the benefit of the other party to the marriage and of the children of the family or either or any of them;

(c) an order varying for the benefit of the parties to the marriage and of the children of the family or either or any of them any ante-nuptial or post-nuptial settlement (including such a settlement made by will or codicil) made on the parties to the marriage;

(d) an order extinguishing or reducing the interest of either of the parties to the marriage under any such settlement;

subject, however, in the case of an order under paragraph (a) above, to the restrictions imposed by Section 29(1) and (3) below on the making of orders for a transfer of property in favour of children who have attained the age of 18.

(2) The court may make an order under subsection (1)(c) above notwithstanding that there are no children of the family.

(3) Without prejudice to the power to give a direction under Section 30 below for the settlement of an instrument by conveyancing counsel, where an order is made under this section on or after granting a decree of divorce or nullity of marriage, neither the order nor any settlement made in pursuance of that order shall take effect unless the decree has been made absolute.

24A Orders for sale of property

(1) Where the court makes under Section 23 or 24 of this Act a secured periodical payments order, an order for the payment of a lump sum or a property adjustment order, then, on making that order or at any time thereafter, the court may make a further order for the sale of such property as may be specified in the order, being property in which or in the proceeds of sale of which either or both of the parties to the marriage has or have a beneficial interest, either in possession or reversion.

(2) Any order made under subsection (1) above may contain such consequential or supplementary provisions as the court thinks fit and, without prejudice to the generality of the foregoing provision, may include:

- (a) provision requiring the making of a payment out of the proceeds of sale of the property to which the order relates, and
- (b) provision requiring any such property to be offered for sale to a person, or class of persons, specified in the order.

(3) Where an order is made under subsection (1) above on or after the grant of a decree of divorce or nullity of marriage, the order shall not take effect unless the decree has been made absolute.

(4) Where an order is made under subsection (1) above, the court may direct that the order, or such provision thereof as the court may specify, shall not take effect until the occurrence of an event specified by the court or the expiration of a period so specified.

(5) Where an order under subsection (1) above contains a provision requiring the proceeds of sale of the property to which the order relates to be used to secure periodical payments to a party to the marriage, the order shall cease to have effect on the death or remarriage of that person.

(6) Where a party to a marriage has a beneficial interest in any property, or in the proceeds of sale thereof, and some other person who is not a party to the marriage also has a beneficial interest in that property or in the proceeds of sale thereof, then, before deciding whether to make an order under this section in relation to that property, it shall be the duty of the court to give that other person an opportunity to make representations with respect to

the order; and representations made by that other person shall be included among the circumstances to which the court is required to have regard under Section 25(1) below.

25 Matters to which court is to have regard in deciding how to exercise its power under Sections 23, 24 and 24A

(1) It shall be the duty of the court in deciding whether to exercise its powers under Section 23, 24 or 24A above and, if so, in what manner, to have regard to all the circumstances of the case, first consideration being given to the welfare while a minor of any child of the family who has not attained the age of 18.

(2) As regards the exercise of the powers of the court under Section 23(1)(a), (b) or (c), 24 or 24A above in relation to a party to the marriage, the court shall in particular have regard to the following matters:

(a) the income, earning capacity, property and other financial resources which each of the parties to the marriage has or is likely to have in the forseeable future, including in the case of earning capacity any increase in that capacity which it would in the opinion of the court be reasonable to expect a party to the marriage to take steps to acquire;

(b) the financial needs, obligations and responsibilities which each of the parties to the marriage has or is likely to have in the foreseeable future;

(c) the standard of living enjoyed by the family before the breakdown of the marriage;

(d) the age of each party to the marriage and the duration of the marriage;

(e) any physical or mental disability of either of the parties to the marriage;

(f) the contributions which each of the parties has made or is likely in the foreseeable future to make to the welfare of the family, including any contribution by looking after the home or caring for the family;

(g) the conduct of each of the parties, if that conduct is such that it would in the opinion of the court be inequitable to disregard it;

(h) in the case of proceedings for divorce or nullity of marriage, the value to each of the parties to the marriage of any benefit (for example, a pension) which, by reason of the dissolution or annulment of the marriage, that party will lose the chance of acquiring.

(3) As regards the exercise of the powers of the court under Section 23(1)(d), (e) or (f), (2) or (4), 24 or 24A above in relation to a child of the family, the court shall in particular have regard to the following matters:

(a) the financial needs of the child;
(b) the income, earning capacity (if any), property and other financial resources of the child;
(c) any physical or mental disability of the child;
(d) the manner in which he was being and in which the parties to the marriage expected him to be educated or trained;
(e) the considerations mentioned in relation to the parties to the marriage in paragraphs (a), (b), (c) and (e) of subsection (2) above.

(4) As regards the exercise of the powers of the court under Section 23(1)(d), (e) or (f), (2) or (4), 24 or 24A above against a party to a marriage in favour of a child of the family which is not the child of that party, the court shall also have regard:

(a) to whether that party assumed any responsibility for the child's maintenance, and, if so, to the extent to which, and the basis upon which, that party assumed such responsibility and to the length of time for which that party discharged such responsibility;
(b) to whether in assuming and discharging such responsibilities that party did so knowing that the child was not his or her own;
(c) to the liability of any other person to maintain the child.

25A Exercise of court's powers in favour of party to marriage on decree of divorce or nullity of marriage

(1) Where on or after the grant of a decree of divorce or nullity of marriage the court decides to exercise its powers under Section 23(1)(a), (b) or (c), 24 or 24A above in favour of a party to the marriage,

it shall be the duty of the court to consider whether it would be appropriate so to exercise those powers that the financial obligations of each party towards the other will be terminated as soon after the grant of the decree as the court considers just and reasonable.

(2) Where the court decides in such a case to make a periodical payments or secured periodical payments order in favour of a party to the marriage, the court shall in particular consider whether it would be appropriate to require those payments to be made or secured only for such term as would in the opinion of the court be sufficient to enable the party in whose favour the order is made to adjust without undue hardship to the termination of his or her financial dependence on the other party.

(3) Where on or after the grant of a decree of divorce or nullity of marriage on application is made by a party to the marriage for a periodical payments or secured periodical payments order in his or her favour, then if the court considers that no continuing obligation should be imposed on either party to make or secure periodical payments in favour of the other, the court may dismiss the application with a direction that the applicant shall not be entitled to make any future application in relation to that marriage for an order under Section 23(1)(a) or (b) above.

Text of Sections 8(2) to 11 and Sections 25 and 26 of the Family Law (Scotland) Act 1985

Note. Section 8(2) creates the general power to make financial orders. Section 9 (elaborated in Section 11) defines the principles to be followed. Subsection 9(1)(a) introduces the concept of a fair share of matrimonial property and subsections 9(1)(d) and 9(1)(e) deal with the time-limits on maintenance – the Scottish equivalent of the clean break. Subsections 10(1) and 10(6) define fair; while subsections 10(2) to 10(5) and 10(7) identify what is and is not matrimonial property. Sections 25 and 26 provide that basically household goods and cash savings (eg from housekeeping allowances) are to be shared equally.

Section 8(2) of the Act provides that the court shall make such order, as is:

    (a) justified by the principles set out in Section 9 of this Act; and
    (b) reasonable having regard to the resources of the parties.

9. (1) The principles which the court shall apply in deciding what order for financial provision, if any, to make are that:

    (a) the net value of the matrimonial property should be shared fairly between the parties to the marriage;

    (b) fair account should be taken of any economic advantage derived by either party from contributions by the other, and of any economic disadvantage suffered by either party in the interests of the other party or of the family;

    (c) any economic burden of caring, after divorce, for a child of the marriage under the age of 16 years should be shared fairly between the parties;

    (d) a party who has been dependent to a substantial degree on the financial support of the other party should be awarded such financial provision as is reasonable to enable him to adjust, over a period of not more than three years from the date of the decree of divorce, to the loss of that support on divorce;

(e) a party who at the time of the divorce seems likely to suffer serious financial hardship as a result of the divorce should be awarded such financial provision as is reasonable to relieve him of hardship over a reasonable period.

(2) In subsection (1)(b) above and Section 11(2) of this Act:

'economic advantage' means advantage gained whether before or during the marriage and includes gains in capital, in income and in earning capacity, and 'economic disadvantage' shall be construed accordingly;

'contributions' means contributions made whether before or during the marriage; and includes indirect and non-financial contributions and, in particular, any such contribution made by looking after the family home or caring for the family.

10. (1) In applying the principle set out in Section 9(1)(a) of this Act, the net value of the matrimonial property shall be taken to be shared fairly between the parties to the marriage when it is shared equally or in such other proportions as are justified by special circumstances.

(2) The net value of the matrimonial property shall be the value of the property at the relevant date after deduction of any debts incurred by the parties or either of them:

(a) before the marriage so far as they relate to the matrimonial property, and

(b) during the marriage, which are outstanding at that date.

(3) In this section 'the relevant date' means whichever is the earlier of:

(a) subject to subsection (7) below, the date on which the parties ceased to cohabit;

(b) the date of service of the summons in the action for divorce.

(4) Subject to subsection (5) below, in this section and in Section 11 of this Act 'the matrimonial property' means all the property belonging to the parties or either of them at the relevant date which was acquired by them or him (otherwise by way of gift or succession from a third party):

(a) before the marriage for use by them as a family home or as furniture or plenishings for such home; or

(b) during the marriage but before the relevant date.

(5) The proportion of any rights or interests of either party under a life policy or occupational pension scheme or similar arrangement referable to the period to which subsection (4)(b) above refers shall be taken to form part of the matrimonial property.

(6) In subsection (1) above 'special circumstances', without prejudice to the generality of the words, may include:

(a) the terms of any agreement between the parties on the ownership or division of any of the matrimonial property;

(b) the source of the funds or assets used to acquire any of the matrimonial property where those funds or assets were not derived from the income or efforts of the parties during the marriage;

(c) any destruction, dissipation or alienation of property by either party;

(d) the nature of the matrimonial property, the use made of it (including use for business purposes or as a matrimonial home) and the extent to which it is reasonable to expect it to be realised or divided or used as security;

(e) the actual or prospective liability for any expenses of valuation or transfer of property in connection with the divorce.

(7) For the purposes of subsection (3) above no account shall be taken of any cessation of cohabitation where the parties thereafter resumed cohabitation, except where the parties ceased to cohabit for a continuous period of 90 days or more before resuming cohabitation for a period of less than 90 days in all.

11. (1) In applying the principles set out in Section 9 of this Act, the following provisions of this section shall have effect.

(2) For the purposes of Section 9(1)(b) of this Act, the court shall have regard to the extent to which:

(a) the economic advantages or disadvantages sustained by either party have been balanced by the economic advantages or disadvantages sustained by the other party; and

(b) any resulting imbalance has been or will be corrected by a sharing of the value of the matrimonial property or otherwise.

(3) For the purposes of Section 9(1)(c) of this Act, the court shall have regard to:

(a) any decree or arrangement for aliment for the child;
(b) any expenditure or loss of earning capacity caused by the need to care for the child;
(c) the need to provide suitable accommodation for the child;
(d) the age and health of the child;
(e) the educational, financial and other circumstances of the child;
(f) the availability and cost of suitable child-care facilities or services;
(g) the needs and resources of the parties; and
(h) all the other circumstances of the case.

(4) For the purposes of Section 9(1)(d) of this Act, the court shall have regard to:

(a) the age, health and earning capacity of the party who is claiming the financial provision;
(b) the duration and extent of the dependence of that party prior to divorce;
(c) any intention of that party to undertake a course of education or training;
(d) the needs and resources of the parties; and
(e) all other circumstances of the case.

(5) For the purposes of Section 9(1)(e) of this Act, the court shall have regard to:

(a) the age, health and earning capacity of the party who is claiming the financial provision;
(b) the duration of the marriage;
(c) the standard of living of the parties during the marriage;
(d) the needs and resources of the parties; and
(e) all the other circumstances of the case.

(6) In having regard under subsections (3) to (5) above to all the other circumstances of the case, the court may, if it thinks fit, take account of any support, financial or otherwise, given by the party who is to make the financial provision to any person whom he maintains as a dependant in his household whether or not he owes an obligation of aliment to that person.

(7) In applying the principles set out in Section 9 of this Act, the court shall not take account of the conduct of either party unless:

    (a) the conduct has adversely affected the financial resources which are relevant to the decision of the court on a claim for financial provision; or

    (b) in relation to Section 9(1)(d) or (e), it would be manifestly inequitable to leave the conduct out of account.

25. (1) If any question arises (whether during or after a marriage) as to the respective rights of ownership of the parties to a marriage in any household goods obtained in prospect of or during the marriage other than by gift or succession from a third party, it shall be presumed, unless the contrary is proved, that each has a right to an equal share in the goods in question.

    (2) For the purposes of subsection (1) above, the contrary shall not be treated as proved by reason only that while the parties were married and living together the goods in question were purchased from a third party by either party alone or by both in unequal shares.

    (3) In this section 'household goods' means any goods (including decorative or ornamental goods) kept or used at any time during the marriage in any matrimonial home for the joint domestic purposes of the parties to the marriage, other than:

        (a) money or securities;

        (b) any motor car, caravan or other road vehicle;

        (c) any domestic animal.

26. If any question arises (whether during or after a marriage) as to the right of a party to a marriage to money derived from any allowance made by either party for their joint household expenses or for similar purposes, or to any property acquired out of such money, the money or property shall, in the absence of any agreement between them to the contrary, be treated as belonging to each party in equal shares.

Appendix 3

Guidelines for Using the Graphs in Chapter 6 for Calculating Maintenance

The first step

1. Start with the net incomes of yourself and your partner arrived at from the principles set out in Chapter 5.

2. If you have children and any of those children have income, add their net income to that of the parent who has their care.

3. Add together the net incomes described in 1 and 2 above.

4. Calculate what percentage your income (under 1 and 2 above) is of your combined income (under 3 above) ie:

> Your income divided by the combined income
> multiplied by 100

5. Calculate what percentage your partner's income (under 1 and 2 above) is of the combined income (under 3 above) in the same way.

6. You will then have two percentages of your joint income – yours and your partner's.

The second step

7. Turn to Chapter 6 and identify which case covers your circumstances. Look at the graph (Figures 2, 3, 4 or 5) for use in that case.

   Remember that although the graphs refer to 'wife' and 'husband' they may apply the other way round if the financial circumstances are reversed; and that where children are involved, the graphs may be used by unmarried parents, or parents who have the children and have remarried, to calculate child maintenance only. So:

(a) In Figure 2 husband should be substituted for wife if she has the larger income.

(b) In Figure 3 the parent who has care of the children and who has less than 50 per cent of joint income should be substituted for wife if it is not the wife.

(c) In Figure 4 the parent who has care of the children and who has more than 50 per cent of joint income should be substituted for wife if it is not the wife.

(d) In Figure 5 husband should be substituted for wife if he has care of the children and has more than 60 per cent of joint income.

8. After changing 'wife' and 'husband' as necessary under 7 above, mark at the appropriate point on the scale on the bottom line of the graph you are using the percentage for wife's (or husband's or male or female parent's) share of joint income as you have calculated it under the first step.

9. Take a ruler and mark on the lines A–B, C–D, D–E or E–F (depending on which graph you are using) the point or points vertically above the mark you have made under 8 above.

10. Again using your ruler, mark the point on the left-hand scale (Figures 2–4) or right-hand scale (Figure 5) which is horizontally opposite the mark or marks you placed on the lines under 9 above.

11. Work out from the scales the exact percentage which the points that you have marked under 10 above indicate.

The third step

12. You will now have:

(a) From the first step above the percentage of the joint income which you have and which your partner has.

(b) From the points marked from lines A–B or E–F the percentage of joint income which it is suggested you should have, including maintenance if it is payable.

(c) From the points marked from lines C–D or D–E the maximum percentage of joint income additional to your own and any maintenance payable or calculable for you which it is suggested can be available to maintain your children.

13. To calculate maintenance appropriate for spouses or former spouses multiply the joint income of yourself and your partner by the percentage which you have under 12(b) above (spouse's income plus maintenance), *deduct* that spouses's income from the result, and what is left is maintenance.

14. To calculate the maximum available to be allocated to children under Chapter 6, Case 8:

(a) If you are using Figure 3, take the percentage figure which you have under 12(c) above, *deduct* from it the percentage figure which you have under 12(b) above (whether or not the parent with the children is entitled to maintenance), and multiply the joint incomes by the remaining percentage. Then decide how much of the resulting (maximum) figure should be paid under Chapter 6, Case 8.

(b) If you are using Figure 4, multiply your joint incomes by the percentage figure which you have under 12(c) above, deduct the actual income of the parent who has the children from the result, and then decide how much of the balance (the maximum figure) should be paid under Chapter 6, Case 8.

Appendix 4

Divorce Reform Proposals

In 1990 the Law Commission published a draft bill proposing radical changes in the grounds and procedures for legal separation and divorce (Law Com No. 192: The Ground for Divorce). The Lord Chancellor issued a Green Paper seeking discussion of these proposals, now to be followed by a White Paper which will almost certainly be along the same lines. They may form the basis of new law to be introduced some time after 1996–7 and are therefore outlined here.

Their essence is this:

1. Divorce and separation proceedings will be started by either or both the spouses lodging a statement with the court. The statement will indicate that they believe that their marriage has broken down and wish to make arrangements for the future. If lodged only by one of them a copy will be served on the other much as divorce petitions are now.

2. The divorce or separation proceedings will then pause for a period of 11 months. During that period financial issues and issues involving any children will be resolved under the direction of the court. There will be opportunities for conciliation. The court may extend the 11-month period if those issues cannot be resolved during that time.

3. Only after the 11-month period and any extension of it has expired will either – or both – of the spouses be free to apply for a decree of divorce or separation. Their application will then include a formal statement that they believe that the breakdown of their marriage is irreparable. The fact of that application will, after the intervening period, be accepted as confirming that the marriage has broken down irretrievably. On that basis the decree will be granted one month later.

4. An existing separation order may later be converted into divorce by similar procedures.

The main differences between the proposed system and that which has existed since the 1969 Divorce Reform Act are these:

1. Either spouse will be able to start divorce or separation proceedings and neither will have to prove any reason to justify the application. Adultery, unreasonable behaviour, desertion and the other old grounds of divorce will cease to figure in the law, though maybe not in people's private reasons for seeking divorce.
2. Matters involving children, finance and property will all have to be sorted out before there can be any decree. Divorce will not be possible until the spouses know the reality of the consequences. In addition, as proposed by the Law Commission, the courts will have power to delay a decree indefinitely if delay is in the interests of any child, or if allowing a decree will result in grave financial or other hardship for a spouse who does not want a divorce.
3. There will be a minimum 12-month delay before there can be any final decree of separation or divorce – allowing time for reflection informed by knowledge of the consequences. Under the 1969 Act the divorce itself may take three months or less, though matters involving children, money and property may drag on for years.

Index